Raising Our Voices

an anthology of
Oregon Poets Against the War

the habit of rainy nights press
Portland, Oregon

Cover and book design by Duane Poncy,
the habit of rainy nights press.

Cover Art by Roberta Badger.
(see note at the end of the book)

to order contact:
the habit of rainy nights press
104 NE 72nd Ave., Portland, OR 97213
www.rainynightspress.com

Acknowledgments

Special thanks to all of the poets who donated time, money and, of course, poetry to make this volume happen, and more importantly, to make a courageous social statement. Thank you also to the many poets who raised their voices against this war.

Thanks to Joyce Epstein, Willa Schneberg, Michael Tucker, Emily Dawn Riley, Lisa Taylor, Robert Hill Long, Steven Shinn, Ingrid Wendt and others across the state of Oregon who organized anti-war poetry readings and gave us another venue to express our sadness and rage.

Thank you to Judith Barrington and Ursula Le Guin for the fine introduction, and Roberta Badger for the wonderful cover art.

Hannah Leah and David Abel organized publicity, poetry readings and proofreading assistance. Patricia McLean handled bookkeeping, correspondence, and editorial work. Duane Poncy did editorial work, layout and book design, and developed the website.

Judith Arcana's poem, "Once I Sat on the Side of a Mountain," was first published in *Exit 13*, #17, 1995.

Joan Maier's poem "Reservoir" was first published in *MR. COGITO*, Volume IX, Number 3.

Carter McKenzie's poem "Prayers at Ratheon" was first published in *The San Francisco Bay Guardian*, 7/31/91

Ingrid Wendt's poem "Words of Our Time" first appeared in *Many Mountains Moving*, Vol. 1, No. 2 (1995)

Dorianne Laux's poem "Cello" appears in the journal *Speakeasy*, Vol. 1, Issue 5 (April 2003). Used by permission.

"Heavy Weather" by David Vest originally appeared as a song on his Trillium Records CD, "Way Down Here."

"Green Smoke" is from Ralph Salisbury's latest book of poems, *Rainbows of Stone*, University of Arizona Press, 2000.

Margaret Chula's tanka "after the ceasefire," is part of a longer piece in *Always Filling, Always Full,* published by White Pine Press.

"Invitation" by Caroline Dunn is from her book *Oris*, published by Copper Canyon Press.

The following poems have also been published in The Nation anthology of *Poets Against the War*: "Cello" by Dorianne Laux; "American Wars" by Ursula K. Le Guin; "We Are Waiting for Peace to Break Out" by Carlos Reyes; and "On the Photograph of a Severed Hand" by Jim Shugrue.

All poems in this anthology are used by permission of the author.

Editors' Note

The idea began at a Poets Against the War reading, organized by Hannah Leah, and held at the Red and Black Cafe in Portland. We suggested exploring the possibility of putting together an anthology. The three of us were soon joined by another poet, David Abel, and the project grew wings.

OPAW is not actually an organization in the ordinary sense. We are an ad-hoc group of Oregon poets who have come together to publish an historical document —an anthology of poems by fellow Oregon poets who responded to Sam Hamill's courageous call to poets worldwide to protest the Bush administration's plans for war in Iraq.

One hundred and thirty-five Oregon poets graciously agreed to be represented in this volume. From poignant to outraged, the voices herein represent a diverse cross-section of Oregonians. The poems come from rural Oregon towns like Joseph, and Merlin, and Winston, as well as urban centers like Ashland, Eugene, and Portland. The poets range in age from 20 to 85.

From novice bard to seasoned poet, we present them side by side, alphabetically arranged, with no biographical info other than age and city of residence, if that was provided to us. Our wish is that each poem speak for itself.

Several poets submitted multiple poems, and, unfortunately, we were not able to publish all of the poems, due to length. We attempted to honor the poets wishes as much as possible in deciding which poem to publish, but were not able to do so in every case.

We want to acknowledge the many Oregon Poets who did not make it into this volume, either because they chose not to, or because, for whatever reason, they didn't hear the call in time. A project like this requires limits and timelines, especially when those doing the work are volunteers with minimal resources. The courageous contribution of those poets to the massive outpouring of poetry against an unconscionable war, is as important as the words of the poets who are included in this volume.

So, here it is, Raising Our Voices. We hope you find it an enlightening experience.

—Duane Poncy and Patricia McLean

Introduction

By Judith Barrington and Ursula K. Le Guin

In January 2003, Sam Hamill, poet and editor of Copper Canyon Press, received an invitation from Laura Bush to a tea party for poets at the White House. He posted his refusal of this invitation on the internet, and asked people to join him in a speak-out movement like those organised during the Viet Nam war. He invited us all to "speak up for the conscience of our country" by submitting a poem or statement of conscience to the Poets Against the War website.

Within a few weeks twelve thousand poets had sent in poems.

Why the tremendous response — utterly unforeseen by Hamill or anyone else? Well, for one thing, writing and speaking is the poet's trade. You're not likely to get twelve thousand people in any other line of work to respond to an appeal to speak. Response is a poet's business — direct response, in words, to the events of life, personal or public, private or political. Poets answer. They make words to fit the situation. Homage or protest, praise or outrage — response is their job.

That's why governments that want silent obedience always hate them.

In the eighteenth century, a great poet, Goethe, said that the highest kind of poetry is occasional poetry, written in direct response to a situation or occurrence. But the idea of a "pure" poetry, somehow "above" any occasions or immediate needs or politics, brought with it the curious notion of the poet as an ivory-tower dweller aloof from ordinary life.

Poetry may indeed seem "out of touch" with a lot of the trivia and junk that fills our lives — because it's trying to get in touch with the real stuff, with what's really going on, what matters. William Carlos Williams wrote,

> It is difficult
> to get the news from poems
>   yet men die miserably every day
>   for lack
> of what is found there

What is found there is a kind of truth that is missing from the 24-hour noise now called "news." Poets try to see what's true, and to tell it. This is likely to put them in opposition to politicians.

Poets don't have any corner on truth, of course. But Shelley's "Poets are the unacknowledged legislators of the world" may mean that the "laws" poets follow and teach are the laws of perception that underlie all ethical actions and institutions, including those of our Constitution and the "truths we hold to be self-evident."

Truthfulness is not all that makes a poem, and much of the poetry written in response to a political or other emergency or catastrophe is hurried and imperfect. But if it's honest, a genuine response, it's useful, it's important to us, here, now, at the bad time. Even if it doesn't speak for eternity, it speaks for us.

Oregon has long been seen as a maverick state. It is not surprising, then that in 1990, after rowdy protests at a visit to Portland by Dan Quayle, a Bush the Elder staffer referred to us as "Little Beirut."

Portland offers a huge array of regular poetry readings: Literary Arts' Poetry Downtown series brings internationally known poets to town; college campuses and bookstores hold regular readings; and coffee houses present wild slam performers, earnest reciters, and those lovable mumblers who pull two creased poems from their pockets for a first public appearance. All over Oregon you can find excellent readings in smaller communities on both sides of the mountains. Independent bookstores have events in Hood River, Sisters and Enterprise. Libraries from Lincoln City to La Grande host local and regional poets, while in towns like Stayton monthly readings in art galleries draw crowds. Poets and their students gather for workshops in Newport, Ashland and Joseph, and cowboy and fisher poets meet in Denio and Astoria.

A willingness to speak up — even to shout loudly — as well as to think and write creatively has resulted in a substantial body of work from Oregonian poets against the war. We follow in the footsteps of William Stafford, the Oregon poet who was never afraid to comment poetically on the state of the world. "Justice will take us millions of intricate moves," he wrote. Some of those moves will be inspired by the words of today's poets.

As Audre Lorde wrote, poetry is not a luxury. Readers turn to it for the comfort of a shared vision and a sense of community. For poets, writing in hard times is indeed a responsibility. Nobody ever said it better than Grace Paley, in "It is the responsibility":

> It is the responsibility of the poet to stand on street corners
>   giving out poems and beautifully written leaflets
>   also leaflets they can hardly bear to look at
>   because of the screaming rhetoric ...
> It is the poet's responsibility to speak truth to power as the
>   Quakers say
> It is the poet's responsibility to learn the truth from the
>   powerless
> It is the responsibility of the poet to say many times: there is no
>   freedom without justice and this means economic
>   justice and love justice ...
> There is no freedom without fear and bravery. There is no
>   freedom unless
>   earth and air and water continue and children
>   also continue
> It is the responsibility of the poet to be a woman to keep an eye on
>   this world and cry out like Cassandra,
>   but be listened to this time.

David Abel, 46
Portland

Pastime

Sunday evening, on the way to the Requiem: the drinkers

at the Turkey's Nest, at Teddy's,
Tom Milano's and the nameless place on the avenue

crowd to the rail of the bar, tilted up
on the crest of the wave to their triangulation

watching the stars,
the millionaires above

Yeah! YEAH!
Look at that pass,
WHAT A FUCKIN' PASS !

Happy Hour's almost over.

This is the people united,
the country at war.

1/20/91

The Interval of Peace

Fragile
          wounds
written
              in anaesthetic

blood is thicker,
blown out to sea, to sink

...thicker than oil,
it stops the heart

and gravity is forensic.

Is it oil or ink on the sand?
No matter.
The blade has bitten,
the hound leaps.

The names, thousands, swell like tongues.

If our words are not as sharp
as the barrels' sweat —

scarred hearts
surgical ruins

betrayed

1/30/91

Bo Adan, 39
<u>Eugene</u>

Pacific Daylight Time

What was it that we had decided? ~ When
The first jet slammed into the North Tower,
We'd slithered past reconciliation,
To dissemble, hissing, in our power,
Recriminations (from each unto each)
For not being support to the other's
Vision in times dreams were well beyond reach,
And instead took solace in another's
Adulterated mythic compassion.
Still, somehow, in either of our resolve
I thought, I yearned, forgiveness would fashion
The presence we once had shown to evolve....
Tremulous, switching our morning news on
As you stormed your way out. Damage was done.

Torturous Silence in Wartime

Say what crime I have committed,
For whose pretense you'd have me whipped;
Where's the gold piece unremitted,
Why must my tongue and wings be clipped?
What defamations will you swear
I have uttered or repeated
That are dishonest facts, or bear
Falsely with those who've been cheated?
Though you would incarcerate me,
To shut my mouth and deafen ears
To the breadth of your treachery,
There'll come a day to pay arrears.
A day will come when ev'ryone
Will curse these loathsome deeds you've done.

An Exile at Home

His vituperative vicissitudes,
Erupting often without any cause,
Eviscerate whatever gratitudes
I have felt toward him at times, because
He declaims with such mean-spiritedness,
Then more, turns each occasion on its head,
Insists that I'm the guilty one, no less ~
And requires my repentances instead!
I just cannot fathom his behavior
(What depths to darkness, risen, manifest
When, willy-nilly, I fall from favor
To behold both eyes of his irate zest).
Although Time won't yet permit my escape,
I must shield my heart still from Horrors' ache.

With Age Comes Wisdom

Will the children who stand
Beneath our bombs
When they come whooshing down

In silence following commands
To release them for Liberty
And Justice and Peace

Comprehend the difference between
Others' massive weapons of destruction
And ours which must now

Liberate them from their lives?

No. They are too young ~
Just children who will never learn
To Grow-Up! as we did.

Gary Aker
Portland

Nascent Tongue

She went to the rally
wet green grass
shy shoes
shoulders hunched brown sweater
braver than most
lost looking
head bobbing with Parkinson's
How does she survive
the onslaught of colors
fighting for the sky

I asked if she was okay
needed any help finding someone
She said she was all right
sure she would meet up with
the people who brought her
I wanted to stay
hear her stories over and above
the crowd drums and chants
for peace
Wandering away
into new fields of ripe Maidens'
smooth brown calves
flex in willow strength
that can't imagine the courage
to keep living over
all the wars and depressions
she's marched through up to

This day
hinged on the lines hugging her mouth
smiled thank you for my concern
maybe too proud

fearful or confused to take my
Help me
understand how they can make up
another war on TV
with a bold Tommy General commandeering
bombers launched from ships
far at sea
and remotely call that brave
when this woman
wanders in wet green grass
and March is so uncertain
even the sudden sun and showers are surprised
to see her standing there
surrounded by the colors shouted
by the thousands who came
after her

Makes me bow to her invincible grace
her unutterable beauty

3/17/03

Joy Al-Sofi, 58
Portland

Message to the Ones Previous/Next on Our List

I wanted to say I was sorry for your situation,
Sorry that I hadn't known what to do to stop it before
Things had gotten so bad.

The news made little mention or comment
Surely they would have called it to my attention
If it had been important.

Yes, slick as rain, red as beets before boiling,
But no one even mentioned that people were dying until
The blood ran that deep.

It was because your leader was bad, he abused you.
Knowing how hard it is to end such a situation from within
We were happy to help.

It is meaningless to cast blame, I hold no animosity
We must move forward together, from where we are now.
It won't be easy for us.

Depleted uranium takes a long time to become inert
Maybe a few thousand years or so.
Careful, don't breath the dust.

You can't fault them for not recycling though,
Americans want our government to be ecofriendly
Even when waging a war.

Be sure to call us when the bombs no longer fall
When you have pulled yourself out of the rubble
After you bury your dead.

I understand that it was hard to ask for our help
But I am sure you will want to thank us
Later, when the dust settles.

We had only your best interests at heart
That's what everyone always said.
You believe me, don't you?

Stew Albert
Portland

Kids

Iraqi children
dead and wounded and terrified
paying painful prices
for Bush Gang's military chutzpah.
Dubya spreading Reagan's Revolution at gunpoint.
Iraqi oil will be denationalized and sold on the cheap.
Heil Hummer!

If surviving Iraqi kids behave themselves
we will give them chocolate
and maybe even let them drive our jeep.

Teenage American soldiers
looting a dictator's palace,
cheered on in the embedded mind and headlines,
doing what was always forbidden,
killing people who piss you off
and stealing their pretty trinkets.
Our kids will also pay a price for this war
when after the homecoming parade
feeling unemployed and unappreciated
they play at Baghdad in the suburbs.

Judith Arcana

Once I sat on the side of a mountain

Once I sat on the side of a mountain
balanced on a rocky mountain
in the tall Colorado heart
small pieces of mountain fell away from me
past walls of gold stone and green pine
but sky was blue all over me
sky was blue all over me
and eagle flew under my feet.

I took this to be education
I took this to the city as a dream
I took this to my bed
and to my kitchen
to eat it, and touch it in the dark.

William Ashworth, 60
<u>Ashland</u>

War Poem

i

What if we could and didn't. What if
all those children's eyes
in countries that we cannot name cried out to us
and we didn't. The children's eyes
are black, the color of mourning,
of fired wood, or of
the sky between the stars
where dawn gathers
but is not yet seen.

This year smells of bombs. What if we could
and didn't. What if we just didn't. The eyes,
empty as shells, are watching,
watching,
where tears gather
but have not yet begun to fall.

ii

Love one another said the man
in the space between two thieves
but the Christians
were too busy for that.
There were far too many souls to be saved, and anyway,
who came to town following him?
Twelve ragged hippies, and one of those
was a snitch for the FBI.
We deloused the pew cushions after they left.

More blood, Father: the first time
clearly was inadequate.

iii

It snowed in Tokyo that summer;
the white flakes whispered in
on the wind from Hiroshima,
and a small boy laughed
at the way the light lifted
from his brother's body
who had been there
and was now coming home.

iv

We mourn for those who cannot mourn;
We walk for those who cannot walk.
The day stands at the brink of dawn,
But sidles backward into dark.

No gun can guard against the fear
That love might labor in disguise,
Clad as an enemy in war,
Clad as a dark-eyed child who dies.

Who rides the black horse of his hate
Needs a wise hand to take the rein,
Calm the wild steed, unset the bit,
And watch the dawn return again.

David Axelrod, 44
LaGrande

Walking Around on the Eve of Another War

Accompanied by Peto, the only dog I couldn't give away
From a litter of thirteen misbegotten pups, Peto
Who tugged at the end of his chain all day
As dumbly loyal to me as patient-hearted Argos
Awaiting the return of his beloved Odysseus, Peto,
Whose name recalls no mythic predecessor
But one of Shakespeare's irregular humorists, Peto,
Who, released now from his own midden heap, pisses
Wherever he chooses — the wheels of a police cruiser
Double-parked at the curb outside the local Bastille,

Then a juniper bush, a birdbath, a stray grocery cart —
I can't keep up with this serious-eyed mutt,
Who is taking a leak now on the shadowy portico
Of the First Baptist Church, where a haggard-looking
Jesus prays in a leaded-glass Gethsemane, knowing
He's failed, awaiting arrest, Savior-eyes turned heavenward
Even though the Kingdom, as He said so Himself,
Is near at hand, even here in LaGrande, Oregon,
Which is a far cry from the New Jerusalem,
Where Baptists eagerly await this Sunday's sermon:

"Mandate from God: Root Out the Evildoers,"
And Peto, too, demands action not rumination,
But he touches my hand with his wet nose,
The true emblem of his heritage, black with a pink stripe
Between his nostrils, a clownish nose that says,
"Hey, come on, Dave, there's work to do," leading us not
Toward the temptations of heaven, but toward
The Kingdom of Stinks, to which he raises not a glass
To toast once more the achievements of mankind,
But a hairy hind leg will do to sprinkle the green astroturf
At the entrance of the Payne and Proffit Mortuary,
Where the blue-lit clock is always approaching the final event,
And the air now fills with a pungent nitrogen-rich steam,
Just kittycorner to the Episca-pelican Church,

Where the lighted sign board declares this week's sermon:
"The Moral Necessity of War," Piss-steam rising again
From the floodlights straight up into the bared nostrils
Of Jesus Christ, who still casts His eyes heavenward,

As though wanting nothing more to do with this
Miserable, unhappy earth, where, just up the street,

The Methodists, too, are not to be outdone, displaying
The very same Jesus, dewy-eyed, easily- condescended-to
Jesus, gazing skyward like a man with a big pain in his neck,
The Methodists promising stern lessons in moral clarity,
The sign below Jesus calling all cars to worship in His name
And announcing the good Reverend Myron Slippy's sermon,
"Iraq and Oil: The Christian Case for a Just War," on which
Peto pisses, too, without any delusions, Peto the Invisible,
True hero of the Gulf Wars, our "wars of infinite justice,"
Peto, an old soldier of the rugged cross, who has just

Taken a long drink from Mill Creek and is trotting toward
The old oak trees Father Frank tied fat yellow ribbons around
(The congregation humming that dreadful tune),
Bows hopeful for the triumphant return of "our Centurions,"
And although the grave old oaks probably don't give a hoot,
They can't camouflage the Savior's face, peeking out
Timidly from the windows of Our Lady of Peace,
That face lit by the combustion of stars and nebulae,
Other, incipient worlds without end —
Amen! amen! —

Jesus, no less than Peto, yearning for
A not-holier-than-thou-life that
For a glimpse of which
He will no doubt have to go on
Casting His eyes heavenward until kingdom come,
Always betrayed, humiliated, and kneeling
Before the absolute silence of space,
Forced once again to beg His Father,
Who by now may be disinclined to listen,
To forgive again what we are about to do.

January 1991, February 2003

Roberta Badger
Portland

Hands of Peace

Take my hand, said God
Feel my breath
Take my nourishment
Hear my song
See me in your brothers' and sisters' eyes.

Walk with me on your journey
though volcanoes erupt
though oceans flood
though cities crush
though enemies rise up
though temptations entreat
though the fingers of fear clutch your heart.

My hand is firm and warm
Feel the heartbeat of life in my touch
Comfort your brothers and sisters
Cry and rejoice with them
Take their hands
and form a circle
Hold fast to my hand and theirs
through this journey called life.

If you drop my hand
you will be lost
If you drop your brothers' and sisters' hands
you will walk alone.

If you hold my hand
and drop your brothers' and sisters' hands
your prayers will be for naught
against many enemies.

If you drop my hand
and hold your brothers' and sisters' hands
you will drown in arrogance
and wound my earth.

If you hold my hand
and hold your brothers' and sisters' hands
my breath and my nourishment
will be upon all my children
and there will be peace.

War and Peace in Prose

War is mankind's failure to:
Accept diversity
Put justice above power
Protect and share the world's resources.

Peace is mankind's success in:
    Trusting in good
    Resolving and containing conflicts
    Turning enemies into allies
    Sharing sorrows, joys, wealth, love.

Stephanie Banka

The Son

If he's your son
He's anyone's.
In this world
he's everyone's
Just as all is part of the one
So is one of the one.
If he's Christ's son
He's anyone's.
Make way
for more of the Christs to come.
Life must forward for all
Not some.
In the end
There is nowhere to run.
We all come from
And go to the one.

Judith Barrington
Portland

Excerpt from
After D-Day, a narrative poem (Canto Three, 1)

> *...unless we can relate it to ourselves personally, history will always be more or less of an abstraction, and its content the clash of impersonal forces and ideas.*
> —*Czeslaw Milosz*

I am thirteen months old. Earth shudders. A flash
across the world burns bodies. Bones light up
as something that has no color turns them to ash—

something that has no scent begins to seep
into cells that years from now will usher in death.
A wave—not sound, not water—begins to envelop

the world, sweeping up traces of exhaled breath
and wrapping us all in its tight, atomic embrace.
We'll crouch under tables; we'll dig ourselves caves in the earth.

So this is how it ends—the face to face
of men in ditches, generals plotting with maps:
these bombs bring respite, but hardly a lasting peace.

Fallout poisons the air—it floats, it drips,
it clings to the maimed; the bereaved breathe it in like gas.
Who can discern its limits, its shifting shapes?

Betsy Barron-Knox, 38
Portland

Good Eats

My Grandfather was a soldier in WWI
He kept a journal during that time
He never wrote down how scared he was
But every entry mentioned food
Or the lack of food
The unfit food
How many days he'd gone without food
The rare occasion when he had
Good food
Sometimes it just said good eats

Claudia Baskind, 31
Portland

3 a.m. American Dream

I noticed how you put American flag mudflaps on your gasoline
    truck
How you pasted American flags in your sedan's rear window
How you printed an American flag on your shopping bag,
How you draped an American flag on a casket,
How you hung an American flag at half-mast,
How you bought American flag boxer shorts
How you lit an American flag on fire, fire,
How you wore an American flag bikini,
And I got an idea.

I sewed a sleeping bag from two American flags back to back.
I made a parachute from one hundred and ninety one American
    flags.
I tied my American flag parachute to my American flag sleeping
    bag.
I zipped myself up in my American flag sleeping bag.
I leapt from a giant Redwood tree.
I fell from the sky.
I landed in a desert country.

When I got untangled from my parachute, people
said, Did you drop from one of those planes
With the American flag on it?
I said, No, I blew in on a trade wind.
People said, Why did you come?
I said, I just wanted to meet you.

Then I took out my pocket sewing kit and we
Made sleeping bags out of the parachute.
We all lay down that night in our blue, red,
And dusty white sleeping bags, and counted
The stars.

Deborah Beaver, 28
Portland

An Eagle

floating like a bird in the sky
soaring on a crystal clear day.
no wrongs no rights
only truth and freedom flying high.

words whisper down saying freedom will survive.
freedom from your fathers and mothers dying violently.
freedom to choose peaceful solutions.
freedom from dictators that wear masks of democracy.
freedom from war, the ultimate terror.

up in the sky the trees still stand strong
giving haven and home.
peace, love and beauty floating around waiting to be called upon.
the eagle bold and strong swoops down landing high atop a tree, all
knowing all understanding, waiting for peace while watching war.

the rain begins softly, a storm in the distance
there are those without raincoats
those without shelter
another world maybe something will change
another world maybe they'll see
war doesn't equal peace
and hate not love
great power is through the soul
it is only there where truth can be found.
the eagle lifts off again soaring high believing peace is possible.

David Bennett, 57
Astoria

Have a war
for oil
and vanity

Quote Epistles
with undebated
surety
that wields
purity
against evil

Send the progeny
of people
in slums
and on farms
the alienated
and hopeless
raised
in poverty
the dropped-out
the indoctrinated
to harm's
path
to do the bidding
of rulers
whose sons and daughters
are safely insulated
and buffered

Propagate rumors
that inject
convenient infamy

Rain
rockets

that don't stain
our hands

Drop missiles
to teach
the threat of wrath
will not be suffered

Disallow as blasphemy
demands
that war resisters
are brave and loyal
brothers
and sisters

Watch resources drain
from your pockets
as your share
of bread
shrinks to crumbs

Too bad
for the slaughters
of mothers
and children
but spare
the oil fields
and the soil

No doubt
our arms are stronger
our aims
will prevail

Deny
the flames
of conquest
might
ignite

a more crazed
generation of rebels
whose
mad
raves
must be kept checked
with tyranny
beyond
religious or royal
lest
they spread
like waves
from pebbles
in a pond
with ever greater reach

Wait longer
to discover
what success
can entail
when news
goes awry

No kidding

Any war
for oil
and vanity
is insanity

Eleanor Berry
Lyons

2002
A Palindrome

> *It's not okay, and it's not going to be okay.*
> —Edward Dorn

Will this year end as it begins,
in darkness, war, and preparations for war—
suicide attacks, ultimatums, bombing runs,
build-ups of troops along disputed borders?

Between this beginning and that end,
the O of loss, howling with grief,
and the O for *other*, despised and feared,
everywhere under suspicion, questioned and held.

Along disputed borders, build-ups of troops,
ambushes, missile strikes, nuclear tests—
in darkness, war, and preparations for war,
will this year end as it begins?

David Biespiel
Portland

Civilization in the Next War

We didn't want to smell the underside of leaves
Out near the sand and the draining rage.
All we knew, overhead, muffled, badly sketched,
Were clouds, like lips, steeped in mist. Serenity
Meant standing with terrible strangers, waiting in line for a train.
Most days so little time to work the last nicotine-
Oiled intimate streets. Who could ever forget
The choral summers, tight-lipped, like steel?
Children still stripped to their underwear,

Happy as tall grass, and ran in the watery universe
Spewed from a broken main—how they laughed
With their grandparents looking tense, squinting, looking on.
The water plunged and shot—the children
Swung like dolls—in and out of the puddles,
The light like metal in the eye. Who said it was a phony war?
Sure as the body must break before it can feel
The rhododendron exploded. The blooms rattled
And flared over the picket fences and the thick
Perennial brick-beds. Just living felt evil.

Spring Bishop, 47
Halfway

In the Stillness

All you people tell your stories,
what you hear now, in the stillness.
The Mother shows us in the stillness
how to hold the Peace.
Her light melts fear raging 'round us.
Only Love abounds.

All you people live your stories,
what you hear now, in the stillness.
The life-carriers for life stand strong
over all the world.
The world suffers our consumption.
Why defend it with war?

All you people here's my story,
what I hear now, in the stillness.
With liberty from our excess
comes justice for all.
All you people tell your stories,
what you hear now in the stillness.

Jillian Bower, 24
Corvallis

today

today 1100 crosses stood on the commons
cold, unmarked wooden crosses
as far as the eye could see

look at all the unborn babies
they said
snuffed out before their time

but that is not what i see

thousands of white marble crosses
marked on a windswept cliff
some bore first names, some last
some both or none at all

rain poured down from grey sky
i stood at the point and
listened to the angry normandy sea

across the rolling field
blood-stained concrete
painted with swastikas
the sign — tattered and
weather-beaten —

do not stray from the path
live land mines present

so many horrid ghosts
echo off those concrete walls
silently
a vigil that never stops
never sleeps

within my breast the fire
beats with an unsteady

rhythm
i see their faces
their lives
spilled out on the cold floor

today 1100 crosses stood on the commons

Deborah Buchanan, 54
Portland

Predator and Prey

The whole sky shakes,
sound fills the air,
and there is nowhere to flee,
the ominous silhouette
coming closer, settling down
over the mud and thatch houses.
It hovers overhead,
an angry wasp,
its reverberating whir
drowning walls and trees,
even the small lizard
under the rock
is shivered in his hole.
Out of its belly flash the missiles,
immense, elliptical, dark
payloads—
each one holding itself
inward and still
in those few seconds of free fall,
then opening out,
giving away its secret power
in that moment of contact—
a fiery blue and orange
and deafening roar
and the world below
disappears.

Lozetta Cadwell, 47
<u>Albany</u>

Look in Our Own Backyard First

War anywhere, anytime is a degrading work of mankind,
brought forth by ulterior motives, no meeting of the mind.
We teach our kids not to fight, that it is never alright to hit,
to have an understanding of one another and have a healthy
    respect to live.
Hoping they will get along with anyone else they meet,
not to let themselves be trampled upon, but how to back down
    without defeat.
Laws are enforced, rules were made for everyone on this earth,
no guarantee when time runs out, is established at their birth.
There is a certain hypocrisy in teaching our kids what is right,
when adults in charge of our own country,
cannot find resolutions without a fight.
So many senseless killings already progressing
    throughout our land,
we try to teach our kids no bullying; then
    forcefully raise our hand.
We need to remember that we should clean up our
    very own backyard,
without trying to pull out a splinter in others' eyes,
a log in our own, explaining the difference to kids is hard.
Not to mention how many will die and suffer at one's hand
    filled with greed,
not caring if peace and values remain, Lord only knows what a
    dirty deed.
Families ripped apart, our country's a mess and all the enduring
    senseless loss,
we teach our kids to listen to others with understanding,
    knowing later the benefits and cost.
War is not inevitable, as someday it will bring
    a spectacular blinding reward,
but it will not be fought between brothers and sisters,
for the "big one" will involve our great Lord.

Brian Carlstrom, 39

when will they learn?

war is death
misery and pain
tears, blood, guts
revenge
more war
when will they learn?

Karen Tommee Carlisle, 59
Portland

In Hiroshima, There Are No Birds
(from Gone to Soldiers, Marge Piercy)

Where once a fine-boned hand
caressed the honeyed crysanthemums into grace
and closed the bamboo blinds against
the scarlet afternoon,
no pine quivers before the sea winds.

Where once a child sat beyond the tatami mat, her fingers
scooping rice and miru weed from a smooth wood bowl,
it is flat.
It   is   flat.
No scrap of cotton quilted cloth remains.
Locusts hum no more.
Behind the eye, mallards wing,
but not across the yawning sky;
irises and herons   melt.

The Children Weep

Photos of children assault my dreams.
A child's leg swirls up from darkness,
a flailing hand streams past.
It is a small brown hand
that led a milk goat home.

They float through the air—
heads without faces, hands that plead and reach
for me like vines whose tendrils snake
around my neck, choking me into wakefulness.
They float before my eyes still, the flat blank eyes
of children in the streets of Jenin, Kandahar and Um Qasr.
Muslim children
huddled together
waiting.

After the smoke of bombs, mines, rifles, grenades
disappears into the innocent day,
they are left, legions of half-things
Inheriting waterless homelands
Where love might never root.

The children weep
night and day.

Judith Catterall, 53
Portland

Excerpt from Episodes on the Edge of Time

On the edge of time
    the mirror mocks
        reflecting moments
            marinated in blood
            seasoned with sins
            tenderly harvested
            from an herb garden of sacred lies.

moments stirred to life
　by the deniers of life
　brought to a boiling rapture
　　each bubble oozing
　　the holy puss
　　of original sin.

the mirror mocks
　as lovers meet
　reeking of carnage
　their feelings shrink-wrapped
　in plastic made of
　melting bones.

the mirror mocks
　as a child is struck
　　stifled
　　silenced
　and the child grown
　strikes back with bombs
　　the circuitry of his being
　　wired to fear.

the mirror mocks
　as suffering is passed
　　hand to hand
　　heart to heart
　　neighbor to neighbor
　and the mirror wonders
　　where is the heart
　　that can hold the pain
　　and not pass it on.

On the edge of time
　the mirror mocks
　　replaying episodes
　　of hallucinogenic prophecy
　　and revelations that breed self-hate
　　and raptures that breed deception
　　　until the mind shuts down
　　　　and imagination fails...

until heaven is never
where you are
who you are
or when...
until the momentum of hope
is stilled
and the self-fulfilling prophecies
cycle through time
the death wish of a species.

Carolyn Chamberlayne, 33
Portland

In Almost Endless Time

It feels like endless time,
Long distance running on a vast summer road.
The long upslope of a hill in the distance.
With every footfall I can hear the grasshoppers whirring
And the shushes of the grasses
And watch the path of cement wave and shine in the long
    stretch.

It's so plodding;
It lasts almost forever.
As long as a family roadtrip.
Just lying in the backseat of the car,
Chewing on a popsicle stick,
Hair lightly stinging the face with wind whips.
Watching the telephone wires trail up and down.
I am mesmerized.
I feel lovely.

Sometimes I even think about doing something else.
I go through the process like a show.
First I wake up,
Then all the scenes from bathing.
Squeezing out the last bit of shampoo from the upsidedown
    bottle.
And then the many acts from eating breakfast.

Peanut butter spread first, then blackberry jam,
Then banana slices, then a sprinkle of cinnamon.
A zillion details that I can go over, change, or keep the same.
A carefully edited story or a tangled and mysterious view.

Eventually, and usually without immediatly noticing,
I do reach the top of the hill on the road.
Again, I hear my shoes smacking the hard surface that I'm on.
And that sound makes me remember the pen in my hand
And see the words on the paper

Margaret Chula, 55
Portland

after the cease fire

after the cease fire
refugees from Chechnya
return to rubble
sparrows weave the hair of children
into their spring nests

Paul Cooke, 48

war and duct tape

war.
what is it good for?
absolutely nothin'
except to perpetuate fear

duct tape.
what is it good for?
too many uses to name
although one might use it to
seal their mind from truly

thinking
about
what
we
were put
here
for.

war?

Jane Cothron, 46
Newport

Holograms

Coherent light refracting meaning
in voiceless memory
showing reality that once existed, forever frozen in a singular
moment

Imagine—
holograms in standing ranks:
The dead—
Auschwitz, Jenin, New York, Tel Aviv, Tiananmen Square,
Flanders fields, Kent State, Armenia, Gettysburg, Kinshasa,
Wounded Knee, My Lai, Andersonville,
Kosovo, Bhopal, Manassas, Chechnya, Argentina.
The dead—
caught in a moment by love, remembered.
Would the living pass among them,
shoulder to shoulder as in life,
seeing abruptly ended possibilities?
To recognize—
soldier boys who never grew into grandfathers,
women raped, killed, dismembered,
children dead too soon—
And think again before killing?
What price the war memorial?

Wendy Counsil

War Stories

1. White Christmas

You have no idea
what it's like, he said, to hear
this song when you're ten thousand
miles from home. And your feet
are peeling in sheets
inside your boots and lizards
have colonized all your earthly goods.
The air is so wet you fear suffocation
and you would sell your soul
for a piece of pumpkin pie.

2. Patrol

When I went out on patrol,
I sat with my back to a palm
tree and buried my face
in my arms. If
I didn't see anyone
I wouldn't have to shoot.
I shot high for three years.
I could not forget:
Thou shalt not kill

3. My Father

is dead. For years, his rows
of medals hid in a box
in an army trunk under a bag
of rock salt next to the water softener.
I would go down cellar to eat
a chunk of salt and look at them sometimes,
and taste dried tears

4. Daughters

Now I look at my Japanese students
and know, beyond doubt, that one
of them is alive because
my father hid his eyes,
shot high over her grandfather's head.
In her gentle brown eyes, my father
still lives.

Shelley Davidow
<u>Pendleton</u>

Would there be War if men...

If God were truly God enough
To just butt in and do her stuff,
She'd set the scene so men would wax
Their eyebrows, armpits, legs and backs.

And in that great communal need
To please their God, men would indeed
Have little time to stir up war,
They'd all be feeling far too sore.

They'd spend the seven weeks or so
(The average time for hair to grow)
Discussing with anticipation
Less painful means of depilation.

We women (with God on our side)
Would then be free to change the tide,
To change the world, to change the way
The laws are made — and we'd display

Our hairy breasts, whilst men might please
Us nightly with their shiny knees.

Lia Denae, 49

Sky Blue, False Star

>Fingertips severed below nails
>painted flame, a sky blue burkha
>steps between song draped trees
>in front of a truck she doesn't see,
>lives to be a moment on the goal line
>of the soccer stadium in Kabul.
>AK-47 aims (not at star striped planes)
>to strike a sky blue mother of seven.
>
>Let light from our gardens golden leaves
>breathe and burn into the opening
>in clouds, into the passes between mountains,
>let it pierce the darkness,
>reach up to the North Star shining,
>shine down on desert children
>orphaned this very night
>by false falling stars.

Daniel Denton, 40
Portland

Activities In Baghdad

>i avoid the deadly triplet
>of military, military & military.
>The vitality necessary to slaughter
>armies transferring aid to overthrown
>reporters. Painted as the resumé of moderates,
>voices of caution compared to the end
>of operative recounts
>of Republican efforts
>of disenfranchised Black Americans
>in Florida. Green light to
>pundit distastes based on decency
>working its will on the world.

As short & medium range
damaged health facilities
sum up the key members address.
As he explores your options,
his weapons of mass peace
bring forward public opinion.
Unjust sanctions of regional
security arsenals by Paragraph 14,
links to oil updated scenerios
(concealed)
sending scientists outside Iraq.

The application of Democracy varies from
time to time. As does the curious
recommendations of mandatory war.
The bottomline of regional domination
is the basic mistrust connected
to the alleged situation.

Senior officials direct assisted cycles
in Yemen, October 2000.

Dan Dillon, 48
Grants Pass

Victory Garden 2003

Gray rain dogs our walk through winter streets
the color of war. Protests stapled
to garden stakes sprout like shrubbery
spiked with finger-paint blooms imploring
REGIME CHANGE AT HOME, DROP BUSH NOT BOMBS.
Every letter growls like flowers
planted gingerly in gun barrels
many walks ago; each announces
the color of dissidence rising,
awakened from duck-and-cover dreams.
Spring will draw strength from these winter rains;
we will draw strength planting seeds whose shoots
challenge tired voices under the bed.

When time is broke

Fall musters the art
of undeclared wars.

Mourn in song how the world works —
love, death, great singing
from major to minor key —
no foolish consistency.

Let spring be a comeback
seeking the wild,
a mind roaming free,
a friendly face in the fire.

2.12.03

Jeannette Doob, 58
Merlin

Merlin Road

Before my headlights merged
with the form in the road,
I saw the truck pulled to the side,
its driver raising a hand to stop me.
A doe lay on the yellow lines, not dead,
the bones of her pelvis or hips,
who could tell, naked and white.

Why speak of deer when land mines
cleave the flesh and yellow canisters
rob children of their dreams?
But there was the doe struggling to stand,
her eyes wild with something
we could not know.

Doug Draime, 59
Ashland

501 Jeans

They bury the dead in Iraq,
children wearing 501 Jeans
made in San Francisco,
California: buried in
Iraq. The president says
we are fighting evil,
the New World Order
president says we are
fighting rampant evil. A
tele-evangelist praises God for
the conversions
happening in Kuwait: tank drivers
and bombers
coming to Jesus,
as death is engineered for
women and children,
women and children wearing
501 Jeans
made in San Francisco, California,
but buried in
Iraq.

(written during the Gulf War in the early 90s)

Carolyn Dunn
Astoria

Invitation

> *Armed drones are mighty weapons*
>   *—headline ,The Oregonian, 11/6/02*

Sit down beside the river,
you chiefs of war,
and take in how
there is no line for three-fourths
of the globe which
you laboriously divide…

only the sound of water;
the sound of water
and the flow of human tears
on the last one-fourth of earth
beneath the drone's tireless eye.
Elusive water,
as you yourselves observe,
there where you briefly sit
at our request,
down at the edge of the weeping
and willow banks of the river.

Marilyn Durst, 65
Florence

The Photo Shoot

The grass cold and wet
mats our feet
clings to backsides
            bottoms
                butts
                    asses

With such a wide range of ages
we each have our own term

But breasts are breasts
varying only in shape
                 size
                    length and in some cases
                    number

The sun is behind a cloud
as we lie in damp grass
spelling out S Peace Symbol S
We listen for the small plane
in the cold chilling breeze

The sun reappears
The plane passes to the east
then passes several more times
before heading north

We form an enthusiastic circle
and wave the pilot off
One hundred twenty-one women
age three to seventy-eight
in the altogether for peace

February 22, 2003, Yachats, Oregon

Carol Easter, 44
Portland

ShrubCo

Junta boy,
on daddy's knee.
Smirks with crude,
complicity.

Lynnell Edwards, 38
Portland

Another Armchair General Wins the War

We have been made ready for this, let's
have it done then. Let's hear the wild roar
of war as it comes flashing into our dens,
our kitchens. Let's see the razor of light,
the whistling explosions, the raw sky torn
open and the thunder of walls coming down.
Let the troops and tanks roll across the hills,
into the fields; we already have them beat.
We are tuned in now for the final hour
and the final views of the abandoned capital city:
the domed palace glowing, the single car rattling
down an empty street, the talking heads in Washington
with their chatty analysis, the split screen banter
between policy analysts, some of them foreign,
the retired generals hired to proclaim
this won't be like the last war. This time we have
the technology, deeper night vision, smarter weapons
with positioning intelligence; low-flying drones
that show us the shape of their maps, the color
of their tents. Only the weather keeps us
waiting, interminable sand that swirls up
in demon columns choking and blinding and
blunting all the lethal edges, the slick wheels.
But the world will turn and take the storms
and the fog and the strafing heat as sure
as it brings us the moon and the sun
each ancient day. We have played
and re-played every strategy, grown frantic
with the patter of conjecture, the hiss of speculation.
We have considered the borders, the likely flight
and surrender, the displaced persons
with their bleeding eyes, their wailing mouths.
We have been made ready; let's have it done then.
Get the damn journalists out of the way.
Tell them the tapes are burning,
the sound feed has been swallowed,
the clocks have stopped to announce
the immanence, the transcendence,
the wild, orange unsinging of apocalypse.

The Bad Man Has Left the Building

these rumors of sightings are tantamount to Elvis sightings
(CNN reporter, April 10 2003)

One said that he was driving down the highway
and he looked up in his rearview mirror
and there the Evil One was in the car behind him,

tall in the driver's seat. And there are sources
that say he is at the home of his sons, or with
his family in the northern village. But no

one can verify his whereabouts at this time. Meanwhile,
they have pulled down his great, black statue
in the capital square and are dragging the head

through the streets, taking their turns
like riders atop a bucking bronco,
waving handkerchiefs or shirts or hats.

They are beating upon his image
with shoes, a terrible insult in their country,
and tearing his portraits in two, clawing

at the great wall-covering posters
and lighting them on fire, so mighty
is their anger. And they are draping

the tanks and battering guns with flowers
and flags and other symbols of praise. And they
are doing that strange dance they do in their country,

chanting and singing and raising their hands
over their heads, white teeth bared. And they are running
away now with TVs, toilets ripped from their fixtures,

bookshelves, plates, chairs, even the curtains and tiles
from the vast palaces where he would sit,
listening and watching, perhaps even still,

as his people splay out like a great wave,
breaking into innumerable frothing bits,
flattened, invisible, against the sand.

Barbara Engel, 65
Portland

Dancing on the Edge

On a bright day in January
I cycled down into the town
to hear a few too many speeches
  about Bush and Iraq

Until at last
  we streamed into the street
and flowed (all 25,000 of us) like molasses
to the beat of many a drummer
drumming on cans or boxes or anything at all
and, because of my Little Lulu mask,
  I danced
at first slowly
behind a Tibetan Dragon swerving in great awe,
and then the beat picked up
as we passed by street musicians
and belly dancers
and folks sitting high on pillars
with harmonicas

so that one almost felt
this could turn into a virus
strong enough to turn all armies
and warlords
upsidedown

Per Fagereng
Portland

Haiku

> George Double-Cross Bush.
> Puissant? (That's French for strong.) No,
> Only a pissant.

Lara Florez, 27
Cottage Grove

We Are the Mothers

> Ourselves enmeshed in history
> the potential: your daughters
> the real: your wives and lovers and companions
> the true
> Your own, the women who birthed
> you forth and now are holding
> From this beginning
> We will tell you
> We will not send forth our children
> into this dark of war
> We will not allow our children
> to be trained to kill another's child
> to be trained to hate another's child
> to be trained to follow unthinking the
> wave of death
> that has been raised by the policies of this day
>
> We will not stand while our children
> are maimed by bombs
> are tortured by manufactured illness
> are made to lie down before
> this great machine of war.
> Our children are all children
> Grown, or conceptual.

We will not stand by and let this
Earth become poisoned soil
steeped in nuclear waste
steeped in blood
steeped in oil.

This Earth is our cherished home,
these children are our cherished own,
they are every dream and love of
our human potential.

We are reclaiming, in the name of
the spirit that surrounds us,
that fills our humanity with the capacity for
wonder and compassion,
In the name of this planet, our Earth, who sustains us
and to whom we must steward in all our contemplations,
In the name of all our ancestors who gave their lives to the futility
of political hatred and imperialist policy,
In the name of our grandmothers who stand behind us and
our children who stand before,

WE RECLAIM OUR VOICES
To say
NO MORE

Geraldine Helen Foote, 52
Portland

Talking Peace and War, October 2002

I don't know, Mom, I mean, he's *crazy*
and who knows what he'll do…and he has
weapons of mass destruction….
My twelve-year-old gains momentum, arguing,
confident that he knows more than I.
He's flung himself across my bed,
watching as I pull on dry socks.

I've just returned from joining hands with thousands
people marching, singing with long lost friends,
talking peace in the plaza
where spirits refused the damp
despite a steady drizzle. As I hang
my wet jacket, I tell him about the day,
heart still plump with hope
and thinking he'd be proud.

We have to do *something*, he says,
as a steady rain thrums the skylights.
Then he adds softly, *don't we?*

I pounce on his doubt.
How will war help?
Answer me that! I say, voice rising,
stopping myself just short of calling him Mr.-
know-it-all, impatient with him for having
bought the headlines, my bright-eyed son.
So you're going to trust George Bush?

As October winds rush our house, I throw the question
at him like an assault, barely pausing to breathe,
recalling the rare afternoon he and I
sat stunned before the TV, while, one by one,
men and women of Congress tried to speak,
challenging the Florida votes, the loser's gavel

rapping them down, history repeating,
one by one, democracy out of order.

Now I'm on a roll, saying how bombs kill
mothers and kids just like us, that first strike
just means someone strikes back.

Outside,
the downspouts rattle, and I try to tell him
what it means to have no clean water,
how children die every day
who have never even seen Saddam Hussein.

Then I see the fear in his eyes,
breathe deep
over the work that must be done,
realize it's raining hard,
and he thinks he knows
the threat to our world
more than I.

I sit beside him on the bed,
pulling the quilt around us,
as though the wind howling
in the growing dark
can't touch us here.

I take out my
fear, lay it alongside his,
like a sword hilt to hilt
on the pillow. I plough
through my doubt, admit
that I'm confused too.

I only want to hold him,
blameless,
safe.

Ila Suzanne Gray, 59
Portland

The New Carissa

Just south of here, the tanker New Carissa has run aground,
broken, cargo holds breached, fuel oil is running into the sea,
turning into black syrupy orbs, leaving tar on animals and sand

They are burning Napalm to consume the oil, smoke
    obliterates sky,
they say everyone is safe, no worse than smog, Napalm
burning just south of here consuming the oil, chemical hero

Doesn't Napalm stick to skin, kill everything? Wasn't it needed
to save our soldiers? but not that naked child screaming on TV
flames and plumes of black smoke pulling at the thin figure
flinging herself forward

School, marriage, children, the Reserve, Canada, jail or war,
choices for a man in 1963, I married your dad,
you, the second born sealed his safety, the war ended,
the dead were buried, there were no heroes
the damaged walk among us when they can

Now exploring narrow streets in Saigon you smile at friendly faces
you write the country is the most beautiful you have ever seen

Hammond Guthrie
Portland

In a Moment's Time
(for Philip Berrigan)

The presses might have stopped in their tracks
Television might have shut down in mid-commercial
The Internet might have gone off line—and

The War might never have begun—
If only for one moment of praise.

But none of this happened—

While those of us who know
And those of you who knew
Silently mourn the passing
Of an impeccable hero.

WakeN and WarN

The last ground zero (re) calling
an endangered species running
the planet on diplomatic sand.

1.25 billion roused and more
to waken and warn the world
to act before the mourn.

Unable to comprehend the horrific
Black Rain skin melting now
the *hibakusha* can never forget.

Diana Gwinn, 56
<u>Portland</u>

Soft Targets

They like the "soft targets" most of all.
Stone-faced pilots
Just doing their job
Raining death from above.
Cluster bombs, brightly colored
Disguised like soda pop cans
Explode in young, tender hands.
Steel shards shot in the air
Rip through a bus filled with civilians

Shattering the supple spine of a 15 year old.
Choruses of talking heads
As if in a trance
Regurgitate in unison
Surgical strikes, smart bombs, deep penetration,
collateral damage
While the war machine plays on and on.
Another church explodes in "Bombingham".
Four little black girls dressed in their Sunday best
Pastel pink and blue
Turned to charcoal burnt flesh.
Police rejoice high-fiving in joy and glee
A young woman their target
Her once vibrant body pumped with bullets
Just another death by cop.
Radioactive metal streams gushing toxins
Hidden in copper IUDs
Invade warm, fertile folds
Poisoning a woman's uterus.
White-uniform clad medical professionals
Employees of the state
Inject death into the veins of a Vietnam War hero
Piercing his mother's battered and bruised heart
On the anniversary of his birth.
A desperate mother begs on the sidewalk
Like frightened baby deer
Her hungry children hover near
It's a hit by U.S. welfare deform
A contract on poor mothers and children of America.

The blood of Palestinian children
Soaks the soil from which they spring
Israeli soldiers, god's chosen few,
Obey orders from Tel Aiv and Washington
"Cut them off and kill them"
Before they grow.

5,000 Iraqi children in 1991

12 years later, now there are none.
Says "Mad-lyn" Albright, Secretary of Hate,

Its worth the price I think, their biblical fate.
A predator man lurks in the shadows
Heartless coward, dreams of power
Steals the innocence of a blossoming girl.
Like depleted uranium bombs
made in the homeland of the free market
Ejaculates contaminated waste into pristine virgin soil.
"Soft targets",
human flesh and bone
really turn them on.

Poem to the Politician

Tell me you false prophets
Heralds of deception
What lessons are you teaching our youth?
To bully the small
To quash the weak
To kill
To drill
To shoot
To loot
Tell me you poli-tricksters
What kind of a world are you leaving our children?

A world of war and death
Of destruction
Of domination
Of despair

Don't you even care
That they will pay a heavy price for your vice?

Masters of war!

Merchants of death!

You're such hypocrites!

Who do you represent?

Sara Halprin, 60
Portland

A Call to Poems

The poems are massing at the border,
arriving daily
from the hills, from valley towns and desert hideaways,
from mountains, plains and beaches,
from all the urban and suburban places,
from cafes, malls, park benches, public libraries and rv camps.

Sent off with a wry grin or a sigh of relief
by poets with or without
beards, curly hair, tattoos, tweed jackets, do-rags, shawls or
    spectacles,
veterans who turn to the next poem, shy newcomers sending
    out their babies,
poets who are also teachers, waiters, fishers, loggers, forest
    rangers,
therapists, secretaries and postal clerks,
even a few, maybe three who earn their living as poets.

A few strong poems,
honed,
poems that slice cleanly to the bone,
are placed to take the frontal waves of attack,
while the youngest, tenderest poems
Take shelter behind the vets, poets
used to the hazards of their work.

Festooned with garlands,
in full camouflage,
typefaces smeared with grease,
helmeted, booted tough guy poems,
barefoot, painted poems that grow from the ground,
their only shield the knowledge of pain,
the poems are massing at the border.

They come armed with words
to celebrate life and sacrifice,
to pay tribute, homage, respect,
to laugh, rage, argue,
meditate, deflate, reflect,
to offer telling details and broad visions, everything
except silence, except denial, except glibness.

The poems are massing at the border
between war and recognition,
come to say that the Other is Us
that I am You,
that we will all die in the end,
that the way we take is the way we give
meaning as well as love.

David Isaiah Hedelman
Klamath Falls

When Will We Realize There's No Victory

The sirens of this war keep on wailing;

The thunder of the drums keep the beat;
When will we realize there's no victory,
In war there is only defeat.

    You got to talk out, speak out, shout out, walk out against
the tides of war
        Insist the oil barons tell us what it is we're really fighting for,
    What it is we're really fighting for, What it is we're really
fighting for

War is not healthy for women, for
Children and other living things
When will we realize there's no victory,
Only the pain that war brings.

You got to talk out, speak out, shout out, walk out against
the tides of war
    Insist the oil barons tell us what it is we're really fighting for,
    What it is we're really fighting for, What it is we're really
fighting for

The sabers and the swords keep on rattling;
As politician preach national pride
When will we realize there's no victory,
In war all our children will die

You got to talk out, speak out, shout out, walk out against
the tides of war
    Insist the oil barons tell us what it is we're really fighting for,
    What it is we're really fighting for, What it is we're really
fighting for

Civil liberties are dying
As the rhetoric starts to fly
When will we realize there's no victory,
How many more widows need to cry!

You got to talk out, speak out, shout out, walk out against
the tides of war
    Insist the oil barons tell us what it is we're really fighting for,
    What it is we're really fighting for, What it is we're really
fighting for

Peter Helzer, 56
Pleasant Hill

War Hero

He lived near 82nd and Stark in Portland and was older than my father.
Sometimes on walks to school I could see his wife through the fence
raking leaves or stacking wood. My mother said not to bother
them because they were private people. "Respect them from a distance"
was how my father put it. But once I snuck off behind their house
where he kept strange pigeons that would circle over the rooftops then
sommersault — ten feet or so — before flapping their wings. His wife
discovered me and said, "Please leave." Her husband followed us
to the gate. He asked her who I was; his words were slow, and a curled
hand rose and fell with each step as if hoisting his knee by a wire. Then
one day I saw him stumbling down the middle of 82nd street. Cars screeched
and swerved. He was shouting, "Tanks! Fire! Oh God! Fire!" My
mother yelled at me to get back in the house. Someone called the police,
but his wife got there first and led him away — both of them weeping.

John Hofer, 56
Salem

A Poem for Mrs. Bush,
Which, I Pray, Will Not Upset Her

How nice to live in USA.
To shower, to eat, and greet the day,
To know that trouble's far away,
How nice to live in USA.

If others hate us what to do?
Hunker down and muddle through.
Or purchase something that is new,
To chase away the mood gone blue.

And if they pressure ever so,
Well then it's off to war we go.
We will have to let them know,
What it means when we say no.

Oh yes war is an awful mess.
And some must die I do confess.
To move beyond this grave duress,
We must do more and never less.

Some children, theirs, will have to die,
And this will make their mothers cry.
War is hard one can't deny,
But it seems to come, by and by.

So I hope they'll understand,
We did not want to bomb their land.
They forced us all to play our hand,
To send our troops to take a stand.

But enough philosophy,
Too grave without frivolity.
Here, we like to laugh and see,
The new day's happy novelty.

How nice to live in USA.
To shower, to eat, and greet the day,
To know that trouble's far away,
How nice to live in USA.

Recitation

Where does fear begin?
In the lie.
How does the lie work?
From within.
What keeps it there?
Plastic and duct tape.
What do they make?
Home-made tomb for the mind.
Real evil.

Untitled

What could be more absurd in the face a terrorist attack
Than a verbal volley of prosody
Lobbed over a deaf wall
To explode on deaf ears?

What kind of fools concoct
Such lunacy,
Carrying out foolish raids
By foot and meter
On the distantly arrogant and powerfully distant?

Disenchanted do-gooders, I think,
Too stupid to carry a gun,
Too dumb to build a bomb,
Too afraid to un-dam blood:
Syllable hoarders;
Syntax builders;
Ridiculous rhyme-makers;
The hopelessly misled
Too dense to disbelieve
That meaning counts.

Heidi Enji Hoogstra, 35
Portland

this moment in iraq

life goes on
but certain things stop.
there is no talk of
college.
or even of a child
growing up.

construction started,
but now it is silent.
they wait.
will it still stand?

a mother is
sliced open
to give birth,
modern medicine
without the painkillers.

warriors for peace,
human shields,
report
gracious hospitality.
one observation haunts me:
missing from
everyday conversation,
plans for the future.

february 12, 2003

Daniel Howe, 49
Portland

The Penis and the Process

It has a simple goal...
to push past all obstacles...
with no delays...
thrusting...
Once it penetrates...
its power is felt...
by both parties...
Force...
Command and control...
planned...or not...

How it has dominated us...
An inherant giant...
pulsing and poised...
ready to perform...

Underneath...
another has been held down...
through the ages...
Yet it births...
life itself...

Here is patience in the process...
unequaled presence...
to tell... when to push...
when to rest... in peace...
residing with wisdom...
in a natural mode...
Her innate understanding...
reveals something unknown to man...

She senses her way is sound...
even though... the outcome seems unclear...
There is pain... apparent torment...
yet absolute certainty...
She may still appreciate the penis...
but remembers... that's what got her here...

Process takes precedence...
in birthing new life...
The passionate projection...
may be respected... raised up...
but held firm...
to support the process...

Now it's time... for those...
in the War-den...
to watch and wait...
for a new way...
to be born...

Todd Huffman, M.D., 36
Eugene

The End of the Day

At long last, we have reached the end of the day.

The world had never known a day so splendid as we have lived.
So bright was our day, so radiant with the tireless energy of
youthful idealism that so few noticed the inevitable advance of
twilight.

Today, as the glory of the day gave way to the darkness of a
moonless night, the dogs of war began their barking. Sadly, they
are our dogs; we raised them; they cannot now be leashed or
quieted.

Let them bark! If only that we may remain awake — sentries for
a new and better day. Watch first that our fatigue not lead into
anger — anger will not shine through this darkness. Only the
light that each of us must become can do that.

Stay awake! It is our greatest act of defiance. Though we may be
tired, and tomorrow may seem a long way off, on this night sleep
will not bring the morning sooner.

Do not mourn over the night that "they" have brought. After all,
there is no they — only us. Always hurrying, we lost track of
time, and track of ourselves. Thus set the sun on our day.

And if there is to be a new and better day, it begins with and
belongs to our children. Hope rests in their hearts and minds,
gaining strength the longer we stand guard against hatred and
ignorance through this night.

What was can never be again. So be the change. Our children
are looking up to us — be the light that illuminates the path they
take through the scary darkness.

At long last, we will then reach the beginning of the day.

19 March 2003

Bonnie Hull, 58
Salem

Bay View

A little past the market,
there's a bench
where you can eat or think.
Usually, maybe, I'd think
about drawing, or about
my sandwich, or the blue blue sky.
On Sunday I sat and looked
across the bay, past the hills,
wondering something new.
If the city one hundred
miles away was bombed
could we see the cloud here, on the bay?
Would the particles look colored,
beautiful, before they tangled
up in our hair and made us sick?
Would we turn inside out?
Would our skin come off
our arms like gloves.?

Bette Lynch Husted, 57
Pendleton

Infinite Justice

If you come to kill us, we will die.
Children will weep, mothers will disappear
in vapor. Old men, young men, teachers. Those
who pray and those who don't. The walls will fall
on everyone, and smoke will fill the lungs
of those who gasp, still breathing, still alive
somehow. And then the sound of words:
Justice. Honor. Victory. The price
of peace. The unforgiven will rise up
to steal the sky again, kill and be killed

for truth. For God in all his names. For power.
For things no one will say. Children will weep
and mothers disappear. Then we will wait.
And when you come to kill us, we will die.

Brittany Hutchison, 45
Portland

Peace Thru Equality

Born and bred of savage ways
Up thru muck and ocean sprays
We have risen since the old days
But,
Now we do know right from wrong
Yet still we imprison and bomb
But only for a few
To steal what's not theirs
With nary a vision
Of sharing with all the rest
For this would mean they'd have
Far less!

Don Hynes, 55
Portland

Olive Tree

The olive tree grows slowly,
whorls of age tightly spaced;
a dulcimer waits
within the wood,
and a song
within the dulcimer;
within the song
a dance
of light and dark,

and at the center
of the dance
God;
God at the center
of the olive tree.

Lynn Jeffress, 58
Newport

White House Blues

hey ms. laura bush what's wrong with emily dickinson walt
    whitman langston hughes

you like these poet dudes that's why you planned a poetry
    party feb.12 in the white house

but now you say you're scared of all those other poets you
    invited

those poets who learned from emily and walt and langston

poets like sam hamill sharon doubiago amiri baraka lynn
    jeffress

martin luther king belle hooks, carolyn forché

afraid they'll come to your house and say things that you don't
    like

well, heh, laura that's what emily and walt and langston taught
    us poets to do

taught us to tell the truth go to the white house anytime we
    smelled a rat

say we smell a rat even if that rat is you

know who

Bully Bush

what in the hell's going on here, man
nothing you do makes sense
you ask hussein to prove a negative
he's got to feel like i do i remember
a bully in the school yard
somebody talking faster and louder than i do yelling
saying things i can't understand i'm so afraid
i can't listen but the bully keeps on screaming pointing
at me like i done something wrong and i know i ain't
i stand there looking around and see all those other kids
who stand there with the bully looking at me, some of them
my friends i thought but they're afraid of him too
more afraid of him than helping me
so i'm lost i shut my eyes wait for the blows
for something i've never done i can't get away from
the schoolyard bully his fists battering my head
his feet kicking me kicking me everywhere
i cover up i roll around like a ball yelling mama mama
somebody help me but nobody does cuz they don't want to be me
kicked by the bully rolling around on the ground that way
what a hell of a thing
remember back
to that bully in the schoolyard you were
either bullied or watching the bully bully
someone else how many times
did you say stop
well it's time maybe the first time in your life to stand up
back off the bully tell him
he can't do that to me or you or anyone
it's time for all of us to stand up and back him off forever

Greg Judkins, 55
Portland

We Love You Mr President (NOT!)

Mr. Ashcroft, every time I see you
It brings back memories
Of that bloated and red faced priest
At our high school retreat
Snickering and hissing
It's a mortal sin to kiss more than 60 seconds
Yet later we learned
He was buggering altar boys
Behind the sacristy

Mr. Rumsfeld when I hear your voice
It reminds me of my neighbor
Who poisoned my cat
Because he crapped in his perfect garden
And pissed on his emerald green lawn
What a good citizen he was
His flag out at all the proper times
But he didn't want any niggers in his neighborhood
That would bring property values down

What can I say about you George
Except I can't watch you on TV anymore
Without feeling nauseous
And something loosening in my bowels
You have destroyed the theory of Karma
That the sins of the father are passed onto the son
But proven the banality of evil
I can only pray one day the illusion will stop
And your slimy lizard tongue will slip out
During a State of the Union speech

Where are you three going to be
When the Shock and Awe campaign hits Baghdad
When the 800 cruise missiles explode in 48 hours
Creating a firestorm of 40 Hiroshimas
And the skin of 500,000 people burns black

As they gasp for air but only get a lungful of fire
As black as your favorite Texas steak George
Is that medium or well done for you Mr. Rumsfeld
Ashcroft, do you have sour cream on your potato

Who shouted your names in vain this weekend
Millions around the world thought of you
They painted your names on signs and placards
They weren't wishing you well either
I remember a boss who didn't like me
And how uncomfortable one person's dislike can be
Can you imagine millions thinking you
With the disdain we feel for murderers and thieves
It has to seep into your dreams
Sleep well guys

Gordon David Kaswell, 52
Eugene

We Are Not a Hive

Soldier ants must kill
But human beings need not
Behave like insects

Cynthia Kimball, 40
Portland

This

They are running ahead specters   in smoke

This is burning
This is dark-winged shudder in air
This is severing   what moved

They are now   cramped around a secret   we will know
someday, too.

didn't we swerve to avoid the frightened cat? didn't
we stop hard?
didn't we shake the ladybug from the newspaper   into the
garden
before going inside to read?

This continuing
This crescendo
This
we could have stopped

it could have been us

who stopped

won't someone put a winged hand   on our burning one?
shaken   over a garden
won't we
        go in peace?

Jane Knechtel, 40
Portland

Warmongers

Our leaders have gathered in Washington.
They paw the ground and snort through thick noses.
War is on their minds like a martini.
Their words as comforting as a bullet.
I am reminded how things never change:
We ask them for tears and they hand us guns.

September 12, 2001

Kristi Koebke
Portland

Casualties of War

Be careful what you wish for, want
or promote
Your method of conflict resolution, will show
in unlikely places
Playgrounds, churches, office buildings
Flint, Springfield, Littleton
Small, soft hands clutching
metal carcasses
Quick to test the trigger,
unusual suspects

If you force this path ahead,
may the trail of children you leave behind
forever weigh heavy on you

Kresque, 49
Chiloquin

War Dreams

I awoke to the sounds of drums today
I awoke to the scenes of war.
Surprised how far I had gone astray
I had thought they were no more.

Amazed I stumbled to the sink,
Ashamed, I splashed my face.
Anger next at this lizard link,
Having lost what was my place.

I cried at the sky, I kicked at the wall.
I fell from the room, too shaken to stand,
Felt anger at falling so short of my goals,
Felt hatred at being only a man.

I punched at the walls and my anger subsided,
I knocked down a picture and smiled.
I never imagined how far I'd been chided,
My path was still haunted by miles.

And as I lay crying, too stubborn to pray,
I discovered I didn't know why or what for.
I awoke to the sounds of drums today,
I awoke to the scenes of war.

Barbara LaMorticella
Portland

There Was Before and There Was After

> *There was and there was not...*
> *—Traditional Arab storytelling beginning*

There was before and there was after.

Every day a before, every day after?

Yes, but "after" usually comes when the broom's
put away, when the rubble's swept up,
when the earth has stopped trembling...

There was before and there was after.

Time's so compressed now, this "after" came
during, when the screens filled with smart bombs,
the crowing of newscasters a door
that swung open to a woman in a cabin,
who walked back and forth in her kitchen shouting—

"I'm so angry! I'm so angry! What can I do
with this anger?"

Jet flames of oil, war planes in waves,
the final extinction of dinosaurs...

Everything happens so fast in this after!

Refugee columns that swarm up the mountain
dark smoke from the mid-east from 600 fires
a dark line the earth bobs on the end of
that comes through a black hole the men fear and long
for—

There was before and there was after.

Now that the tide of war planes is out,
What shore are we on? What shore is this
that we walk on in this after?

Frogs of War

So now the frogs of war are croaking
from their pond of fire
and all the haters of peace, emboldened
croak back

They have only two notes:

Kill   Take
    Kill   Take

John Ashcroft Orders the Bare Breast of Justice Covered

he must want to
stop   jiggling
  wipe out round get
                total control   costs
more zeroes

than anybody can   ever
possibly   pay

        so everyone ends up
totally   (dead)

Dan Larson, 33
Portland

If words and ideas proliferated faster than bombs and propaganda

There would be more scenes like this one.
Remember the student who stood in front of a line of tanks
    in Tiananmen Square.
You could tell by his posture he would stand ground.
When the tank tried to go around him he moved
in front of it again, waving his white sweater like a toreador.
He climbed up on top of the tank before they stopped him.
What did he say to the soldiers inside when he got there?
I wonder whether he's dead now or in prison.

And, just like those days when democratic reform was crushed
    in China
when a million people thronged a city square
I know the whole world is watching you now
and it makes me want to lay a poem at your feet,
a poem as daring and beautiful as that Chinese student,
to stop your war of terror while there's still time.
I want to place a poem in front of your tanks,
write in the sky ahead of your bombers,
drop poetic leaflets on the White House and Pentagon,
covering your foreign policy propaganda
with a snow job of my own.

Cynthia Lauinger, 31
Portland

War in December

Why would anyone wage war in December
When the world is cold and already weeping?
The sky sick with sorrow
Wet willows
Trees bare
The leader of our country wears a long black cloak
The tank is ready; they are together.
Maybe it's bright and warm over there
Where it's hot and dry, as they wait for bombs to crash from
    the sky
It's inconceivable why anyone would care
At this time of year
To gather their artillery in the cold and the wet
What force drives one to kill
While the rest of the world is living,
While a cat cozies in the corner in her basket,
Her sleep undisturbed,
For now.

Dorianne Laux

Cello

When a dead tree falls in a forest
it often falls into the arms
of a living tree. The dead,
thus embraced, rasp in wind,
slowly carving a niche
in the living branch, sheering away
the rough outer flesh, revealing
the pinkish, yellowish, feverish
inner bark. For years

the dead tree rubs its fallen body
against the living, building
its dead music, making its raw mark,
wearing the tough bough down,
moaning in wind, the deep
rosined bow sound of the living
shouldering the dead.

Jennifer Laverdure, 33
Portland

Opportunity in Crisis

I.

This is the end of capitalism
As we know it
The day those planes crashed
Into the physical symbols
Of US global imperialism
And the military might
Used to conquer new markets
Our world changed forever
This mighty behemoth
Is not immune to
The tools of destruction
The kind it renders
In the name of
Profit
The images of desperate men and women
Jumping from the World Trade Center
Are burned on my brain
Passengers jumping from
The sinking ship of this economy
The blood spilled
By US money in
Nicaragua
El Salvador
Chile
Became our blood
The stench of the felled towers

Smelled of cities in
Vietnam
Yugoslavia
Somalia
Iraq
Hit by US bombs
Fear swelled the nation
Like a new bruise
Who are the nameless
1000 men and women
Jailed for their ethnicity
In 2001?
All the while
We are subjected to
Post-trauma marketing
Commanding us to
Patriotically shop
These are the last convulsions
Of a dying economy

II.

It is not the end
Of our multi-hued
Resistance
From the WTO
To the FTAA
Men and women
Protest corporate crooks
My Black co-worker
Will not send her son
To war
She says her life
Wasn't worth anything
To Supreme thief Dubya
Before September 11th
And it still isn't today
Palestinians
Throw rocks at tanks
Americans
Australians
Germans
Pakistanis
Take to the streets
Against this

US-brewed jihad
Barbara Lee
Votes no to war
Enron workers sue
Afghan women
Hold classes in secret
Mumia is still alive
Cuba exists
We are rising
To our crescendo
Our insurgency
Can be the final note
Of the US
Crumbling empire

Hannah Leah
Portland

Purse Strings

men running businesses
(as countries?)
pull the strings open
drop in viscous drops
poison a nation

while war-smoke screens
unseemly plans
for wild refuges
and unsuspecting wombs

Ursula K. Le Guin
Portland

American Wars

Like the topaz in the toad's head
the comfort in the terrible histories
was up front, easy to find:
Once upon a time in a kingdom far away.

Even to the dreadful now of news
we listened comforted
by far timezones, languages we didn't speak,
the wide, forgetful oceans.

Today, no comfort but the jewel courage.
The war is ours, now, here, it is our republic
facing its own betraying terror.
And how we tell the story is forever after.

Peace Vigil 3/03

The candles flickered in a circle,
behind them faces
full of shadows, behind them
darkness, mild rain, plum blossoms.
Spring night in time of war. A big man
with a big ragged backpack
wandered into the circle and stood
looking around, till somebody
spoke to him, somebody gave him
a candle, somebody lighted the candle.
Then he sat down on the wet pavement
right in the empty center of the circle,
He sat huddled up over the candle,
holding it in one hand and holding
the other hand over it to get warm, and then
he would change hands. Now and then

he looked up around the circle
of candles and shadowy faces and silence
and his look was mild and puzzled.
When the circle turned into people
going home he still sat there
in the rain with his candle.

Timothy Leonard, 52
Eugene

Basra, Iraq, 1985

Among dust storms
rising offshore
there is a specific attrition

Rusty oil tankers aim
bows at sunset's burning edge

Gravestones
accept wind's whisper
historical elements

Casualties wait patiently
for a hand to skip them
homeward

Solders' swollen feet
approach water border rendezvous,
waiting tanks spit fire
baking flat Arabic bread

Mother bends her way past bodies
looking for a son
in twilight's final gesture of futility

The wholeness becomes
an attribute of attrition

Shortwave Reception

Light,
Reflected by falling
Oil stocks on exchange,
Strike of the pen
Voices from prison breath
Concise

Northward,
Reeds and marshes
Welcome young martyrs,
Their holy quest a liberation
Of religious/political foundation
Concise in decay

Spring,
New growth, morale is high
On frontlines.
Human waves form,
Assault reeds and marshes.
Nature bends with wind,
Under falling weight.
Youth, caught in life's crossfire,
Destined for statistic chart and
Body count
Laments

Wailing sirens,
Voices all a warning
For the light,
Concise and final

Kuwait, 1987

<u>Valkyrie Liles, 29</u>

Dissent Now!

Our alcoholic cowboy is intent
On ordering death
As if it were
a stack of flap jacks.

While home on the firing range
Citizens must buy larger cars
Watch more football
And fly as often as we can
To demonstrate our courage.

Lovers of freedom,
You are being mocked
In freedom's name.

Our values are being turned into
Gooey spreadable hate.
Our compassion has been limited
By fear.

We must not let apathy be
America's number one disease.

Find true courage, find your voice.
At the top of your lungs and
With whatever means,
Dissent now!
Oppose the Bush Regime.

Lynn Balster Liontos, 59
Eugene

The Dove of Christmas

You know we needed you,
a soaring statement
in the sky, purpled by passion
we've all felt for dawnsong,
those warring voices
pitched in perfect pattern,
flying low now above the watery
terror of ground,
and branched straight
at the beak of hope, you lift
your feathered grief
(injuries we didn't know
were ours and ours alone),
and fragile as the smallest
arc of life,
pluck
peace
from that storm-shelled
wreath of days.

Robert Hill Long, 50
Eugene

911

What force of will emerged from us and grew so tall
it forgot the story of the tower of Babel?
The 911 call from the core of the rubble—
that weakening cell-signal —was this the still, small
voice we failed to hear too long? Now we hear it fail.
Now in houses dark as the inside of a bell
thousands of phones ring unheard, unanswerable.
The rest of us rewind the moment the sky fell,

when the unthinkable beings—part suicide missile,
part punishing angel—wing through the glass and steel,
and pillars of trade collapse: clouds of fire and hail.
That pall of mourner's ash covers us all. A bell
tower lies fallen, felled with terrible skill. Stand still.
In your heart you can hear the whole continent toll.

9/12/01

Aces & Eights

What's breaking up in midair is not a mirage: mirages don't carry
passengers. Think of desert air, updrafts of drought and heat thinning
out among intercontinental jet trails, the noiseless nerve-patterns
of microwave and shortwave. Countries trade not only tourists and
goods, but also rumors, weather reports and threats.

Imagine a game of skill and nerves played in this airspace: call it
eight-ball with a ground-to-air missile as cuestick. Assume live
worldwide coverage of this game, with god's million-eye sky-cams
zooming down to promise that no detail will be lost: neither the
crack at the base of the cooling tower, nor the pentecostal tongues
of the antiaircraft batteries. Neither the Jewish-American princesses
falling, naked in their best high heels, toward the Dead Sea, nor the
khaki ballet of Islamic infantry among oversexed oil rigs.

If the Eiffel Tower spouted oil, or if liberty's torch was fueled by
something other than gas, then the desert sky might not be filled
with Phantoms and Mirages trying to catch the naked ladies as they
fall. Shoot a plane and the plane bleeds fire; shoot a country and
the country bleeds oil or money, depending on which language its
terrorists speak. The prayers of muezzins atop oil derricks, and of
evangelists multiplying like spirochetes in the Statue's noble empty
head, fly through the ozone like blue snakes of the apocalypse,
cancelling each other out.

The only prayers that get through are the prayers of those ready to
die or unwilling to be born, voices pitched too high to be heard by
anything but god, the audience of one to earth's violent choir.

This country's language is profit and debt compounded in the way oxygen and hydrogen combine to make water, water which can be drunk, dammed, channelled, purified, poisoned, used to torture, sprayed on anything that threatens to blow. Water is the most beautiful word the desert knows. But we're not talking about water, water is not what we're pouring into the desert. Nevertheless the desert is blossoming—petals of gunfire, petals of flesh, petals of twisted armor beside slick black lakes—and the drinking-birds dip their iron beaks into whatever the sand soaks up.

As for the language we use, it survives midair collisions with history and speculators flooding the market with foreign imitations, in fact it sustains them. It stays as green as the old days, days of the republic. It could drown us except that we know how to dam it, channel it among our tributaries.

But enough spills over that we can use it to place endless bets: whether the next space shuttle will explode, whether this or that Arab will outlive his handful of dynamite, whether god will drill eightball earth into a side pocket of the Milky Way. We're holding the bank and the cards and the IOU's: don't bet against us, don't try to bluff us again—you could crap out, lose it all. You could end up holding the dead man's hand.

Joan Maiers

Half Life

How many animals
perished
in the Chernobyl letdown,
not to mention humans
or flowers?
the same iris I view
at Augen Gallery *
lies fuse-petalled in Kiev.

In my front yard
the magnolia is hot.
Snow feeds it
slurries of rain.
Each May, cottonwood drift
drops its net
shoulder height, showers of atoms
catch the soil by surprise.

Life under fire—
is it any different in Dublin,
in Caracas, or in Yucca Flats?

Clouds carry traces,
life wild and domestic.
How will we know when
to turn out
the lights?

*prints exhibited by Royal Nebeker

Reservoir
April 1987

In Memory of Ben Linder, April 28, 1987

Sprayed across the courtyards,
flowers of Matagalpa
open their valves.
Lavender mists rise up
like moisture from asphalt.

Once again blossoms
fall from the mothers' hands,
scaphoid shapes upon the graves,
an act that mourns the living,
the angles of their faces
so sharp they scrape.

One might expect
to find him there now,
curled under the carapace of diesel
or waking from a dream:
a snake crawling inside
the netting over his bedroll.

In a local northwest home,
I knew him only by a set of clothes
left in storage,
his worker's uniform,
denim, flannel shirt,
rosebud boots, trailwest parka.

Now, candles of our chestnut trees
burn without caution
around northern storage zones.
In a day or so
their clusters will burst vermillion
in the sun.

Colleen Martin, 66
Portland

How Long Does the Pain Last?

How long does the pain last?
Forever

It was February 21, 1945.
On that terrible day in the Pacific
A war killed my brother and
My life was changed
Forever

His death made my parents cry.
It stilled their joy and muted their laughter.
It stopped their singing.

War took their only son away
Forever

My adored brother was gone
And I was left with nothing but
Memories and the pain
That will remain with me
Forever

And later, old men sat at a table
And signed papers and said it was over.
But it wasn't. Not for me.
I still hurt and will cry out against war
Forever

W. Jason Mashak, 30
Portland

UN Council Transcript

"America, you're young, prone
to tantrums. You were naughty
and nine eleven was your spanking.
Now pick up your mess and go
back to your room. And stop
watching TV, and do your homework!
Look at your room — it's a mess.
You have no business coming out of it,
at least until you've cleaned up
that smell and put fresh water in
your fishtanks…Do you understand me?
Do you understand anything I've just said?"

Dumbya the Elephant

I looked at the man's nametag. The letters spelled
"XJ4DRC918SZMLZ18B6RT." I could've sworn my El Camino
displayed the same sequence for a serial number.

The man, I'll call him XJ4DR for short, handed me a document marked "TOP SECRET." I scanned the page with fervor. A concept excavated my eyes, a vision breached, then sanctified by C-section. One sentence waved colors at me from atop a radio antenna. It read:

"Living in one's own country, never having been elsewhere, and willing to drop bombs randomly beyond the borders of one's own visibility, makes the kind of Amerika this administration will force our moral opinions on, biding the collective State to do our will."

In the margin, near the bottom of the page, a sloppy hand had scribbled "This'll help us with Daddy's Nue World Oilder."

My eyes scrambled back to their caves, freaking out as the fan chopped through the manure. All around me schools were exchanged for tanks. It was up to the book clubs to save us now.

David Matthews, 50
Portland

I Would Far Rather Listen to Corelli

I would far rather listen to Corelli
Than to think the thoughts
This day demands I think,
Read a good whodunit
That demands little of me in its offers,
Or stand on some bank of sand
And watch a lazy river flow
While clouds above drift past
Unheedful of the clamor below
And feel a gentle breeze on my face
Like fingertips of flowers
Than to contemplate the horrors
That dawn this day before us.
Called away from contemplation

Of those themes I love best,
On a midnight that is anything but clear,
I compose a poem because that is what I do,
Such a tiny thing next to all this war
And rumors of war and so much living and dying,
A few grains of sand hurled into the wind
To be blown back into my face.
A poem is such a tiny thing
To throw up against machinery of war
Thrust forward with such force
By evil and greed and fear and stupidity
And, yes, too, by choices made
By women and men of honorable intent,
Forced to choose from possibilities
Each one tinged with evil and fraught
With peril for innocent and guilty alike,
On a midnight that is anything but clear.
That things will not turn out
As we foresee or hope
Is all the certainty allowed us,
We poets composing our little poems,
The way lighted by those themes we love best
And trust that it counts — for something.

M. F. McAuliffe

Crucifix V

Take and drink ye all of this:
My blood black with lies
my lies black with blood.

Robert McDowell

Greed

I got out of bed feeling sick of the greed in the world.
Aren't we called to be saints?
Don't we die to be angels?
Prowling through my winter rooms I plan
Offensives against the overeaters,
The politicians, media morticians
And smug over-achievers; parents
With no time for their kids,
Teachers fixated on pensions,
Droning their dimwitted lesson plans.
I think about things I can do
To the tax assessors, the boom box blasters,
The euphemistically named Humane Societies,
The piggy-piggy major leaguers, Intolerance
That would herd its opponents into ovens if it could.
Should we target road crews standing around like statues,
Office workers making a day of the task
Their mothers and fathers would have finished in hours,
The mindless blobs behind automated phone systems?
Why not? Don't you feel greedy for retribution
When you hear the word? If not, keep going.
If it goes on like this, you'll get there,
Sick, sick, so sick of it you'll want to do something,
Anything to change it.

For the Love of You

I forgive white men in power their fat portfolios.
I forgive the accountant auto makers who deny us
The 230 miles per gallon engine. I forgive overworked
Grade school teachers who ridicule student
Drawings and high spirits, school counselors
Pushing trade schools, and the little dog
That never died and never stopped yapping.
I forgive the Dodgers their dismal performance in the '90s.
I forgive interruptions, field bagpipers playing indoors,

Police waving their guns and batons,
And women who lost interest, went nuts, tore money,
Trashed rooms, and silently suffered emotional abuse.
I forgive friends some for using me, some for excusing me.
I forgive the church its buggering and cover-ups,
Poor neighbors who neglect their pregnant mares,
The Fundamental Right though they be fundamentally wrong.
I forgive children who taunt their pets, ignore parents,
And taxpayers who refuse to fund schools. I forgive
Father and sister for leaving too soon, and You
For imposing a time limit on what we're supposed to do down
   here.
I forgive because a sweet prayer caught me, because
My faith is strong, even in its hurricane of doubt;
Even though at times our great, gray world seems
To offer not a single reason for good faith, I believe.
For the love of You I forgive You, Even You,
On high, invisible, inside and all over what we say and do.

Catherine McGuire, 47
Portland

War Nerves

A puppy's anxious crooning
slithers through the glade, answering
the jets' growl above; the martial drone
that sets my teeth on edge — is this
the moment? Like the squeal of brakes
before a crash, descending notes
raise panic in shockwaves up my spine.

Like acid in the stomach,
war spreads its poison
in my life. Not close, but
corrosive — as hostage to the
greed of the rulers of my country,
I can only howl and rage

while they tell the world
that I agree with their plans.

What will stop them?
They plan as if
they will not pay —
and it may be so.
We will bear the brunt;
like medieval peasants
we are being used
and tossed when done.

They live their lives as if they could
conjure "instant replays," change the score
and undo miscalculations.
They live as if they thrived on pixels,
could ignore our physical danger
and reboot if a glitch occurred.
They don't believe in end game.
If only we could get them
hooked on "Ultima," so
they will leave us alone.

Legacy

Shouldering the day, the weight of
neighbors' words, rumors —
the talk of war between fresh-hung sheets,
the taste of fear in the bread.
Take your heavy heart indoors;
lock it in the cupboard, stored like grain;
those who search for traitors
will spot it soon.

Civil war above; sun outwits cloud
for now, but the scene will shift
and neither side can win.
The curtain bunches in your hand
like the family line; folds and shadows.
Stare from the window; the muddy ground

won't tell what it knows. How this portentous
feud has lived, generations like dazed
mayflies in its grip. It will come.
But for now, the rising bread
is a legacy, and you will chop it
for children's hungry mouths.
War and birth are interleavened in
your mother's mother's bones, carried
far beyond her life in questions
that we've asked forever.

Boys like saplings sway as
the storm builds. How eager, they!
You look beyond at felled oaks,
another legacy; your roots are tangled
in the blood that soaks the ground
and births each bitter generation.
Blood for blood, a path so old
that source and destination both are lost —
but you know only the daily steps:
bread to table, cloth to chest, heart
to market, looking for — what?
Well, not answers, anyway.

We have stood by doorways, gazing out,
our mothers' shades behind us,
the children already far in the fields.
We are the doorways our families pass beyond.
Wed to the unending strife, we raise
our youth for the tempest, feel the storm
in our bones as we carry the day
in heavy, rising hearts.

Carter McKenzie, 42
<u>Dexter</u>

Prayers at Raytheon

came after the National Anthem. Beneath the flag
the President's wife wiped her eyes again and again,
a medical problem. Her husband stepped up to the podium,
pointed at a familiar face, clucked his tongue
with gee-whiz affection. "You guys are great" written
all over his face. No futuristic movie
could have done better than this, Mom and Pop under a steeple
of Patriot Missiles, a white-haired lady holding a handbag
supporting the lanky grin of an oilman. They are here to thank God

for Scud Busters, Star Wars made possible by the folks who worked
through Thanksgiving, and, with a respectful pause
through Christmas, he said, made possible
by the folks who were right all along.
42 launched, 41 down, a winning game
against weapons devoid of points
other than destruction. What a vision, the blackout
of attacks against innocent cities. Our argument
is not with the people, he said, as if the existence
of Strategic Defense could eradicate
statistics not worth mentioning

bombs designed to fall
through walls of concrete before exploding, the memory
of a boy in which he wakes to a burning blanket,
his mother formless beside him.

Meanwhile, the President's wife untucked her handkerchief.
The President waved, and thanked the minister
for his lovely prayer. What could be better
than Raytheon, this Gothic archway
echoing with praise.

Patricia McLean, 50
Portland

if the sky falls

it's not about being white or not white
european or african, chinese or aleut
not about being brown and mediterranean
not about ancient civilisations fallen
on hard times
nor about despots and devils
not about god and new nations
teenage nations all puffed up with self
it's not about babies dying (though babies are dying)
not about dresden revisited
not about hiroshima or nagasaki or my lai, kuwait
not about who threatened whose daddy
not about who used what hideous weapon on their own / his own
nor about who supplied the hideous weapon used on…them
the ones over there

from the sky from skyhigh there is nobody below
if seven bodies fall from the sky everyone sees them
if the sky falls on seven thousand
if seven thousand bodies are lacerated, eviscerated
if seven thousand worlds are disappeared
if seven thousand once were dreams, laughs, late night tea
early morning prayer, if seven thousand ceasing cease
down there on the brown earth against the brown hills
by the brilliant sea are buried by carpets of bombs
who will see? How do we name seven thousand names
how do we learn to pronounce seven thousand names
how do we learn to follow the days of their lives
what if there are seventy thousand, seven times seventy thousand?
how many make too many?

six million?

Carolyn Mills, 54
Oregon City

Waiting for War— February 2003

In my dreams we're in Algiers
and the prisoners hang from hooks while
they're tortured. We are the French and torture
is the only way, but the rebellion never stops.

Every day's the same. Eventually
the little that can be told is told.
The torturers smoke wearily in the hall,
horror reduced by repetition to blank boredom.
In the graveyard the freshly dug earth has
a rash of weeds. I wake in the night imagining
my hands are red.

Kelly Mitchell
Portland

The War Creeps Into Everything…

the war creeps into everything
even the biscuits
as they rise to resist the inevitable,
fall…

terror produced tv shows
push capitalism down
poor people sucking fantasies
worldwide while

seven billion souls
rise to grasp ancient throngs
of baby ET super clones
re-emerging

Koreans don't pass inspection
taunt the war monger
who won't even speak
of new year's resolution

perpetual war shakes the sand
under Iraqi moons
people waiting for death planes
hold rifles to the windows

we wait too, unconvinced
stressed into virtual spending
IT is all rising and falling these days
like biscuits...

self-righteous fools with weapons
point poison justifications
at future soldiers watching
previews of ww3 on mtv

December 29, 2002

Deborah Narin-Wells
Eugene

So That the Trees Don't Hear

When my son begins to argue
I want to tell him Stop!
I want to lead him outside
where the stars wait with their light,
where the Big Dipper hangs
over the apple trees we planted
when he was small,
and the owl calls from the quiet
weight of the woods.

I want to remind him
how all things are connected
beyond the fears of this world—
the oak and the thrush,
each word he utters.
How once when I was angry
he told me to whisper,
so that the trees don't hear,
and tremble their grief
into our lives.

Birgit Nielsen, 42
Portland

Forced Persuasion

In a time when there was no war
No one came to my home and tried
To convince me that war was peace
But with war as a constant
Who can remember peace
So who am I to argue?

He is terribly persistent
His body leans
His spit flies
As if it were all that important
To convince me
But for a man who used to
Have his finger on the nuclear button
For the pre-eminent patriot
It is unpalatable to eat
At the house of one
Who does not see the beauty of forced persuasion

This is the greatest country, he says
If only everyone else woke up, he says
To see that we have their interest at heart.

While his heroes hurry up and wait
While his heroes fly overhead
While his master gang plans precision strikes
Collateral damage and preemptive world dominion
The civilian cowers, he imagines
Pleading
Bomb me, please
Deliver me from ignorance
Redeem me into your capitalist empire
Kill me in the process for
I am worthless in your presence

This is the greatest country, he says
We are a peace loving nation
We will bomb you until you get that
Into your ignorant head

Amanda Nordquist, 25
Portland

the power of words

words are silent walking down the street
occasionally a quick acknowledgment to someone we meet
in a world of such misery and grief

why the constant hustle to be that person the world wants us
    to be?
Who is distraught by the games the government plays
with the controls in hand
a video game war
derived from nepotism
where the hell are these people's heads…gallivanting through
life with an antenna?
the media is full of euphemized shit
soothe our minds
we
read

        between

the lines
and cover our ears
the car in front of us reads; ignore the environment—it will
just go away; I love my country but fear my government; has the
love of power overcome the power of love?…words words
words are all that we have
take your words and make them your stand.

Diane Nova, 56
Portland

Heart and Desire
A Peace Prayer

    This is my heart's desire
    To bring what needs to be brought
    To wish what needs to be wished
    To love what needs to be loved
    To share what needs to be shared
    To hold what needs to be held
    To release what needs to be released
    To join what needs to be joined

To heal what needs to be healed
To sing what needs to be sung.
It is my desire
To celebrate all of life
To be a light in a darkened place.

Joan Peterson, 63
Applegate

Centerfold

They could be sea lions beached
on the sand worshiping the sun
except that it is raining and they are small
in the photo, like lizards, some bodies
larger than others, but each one stretched
into a pose, calm and relaxed. At first glance
they might be pieces of driftwood, gathered
by children to spell out a name, but wait,
look closer, they are bodies, women, lying
feet to head, revealing breasts
and pubic hair, fifty women at ease
on Love Field spelling the word, PEACE.

Figures of speech they rally against war.
Mothers of sons who were raised
with sounds of waves washing the shore
of sea birds calling at the end of the day.
They are mothers who taught their children
to love. They are grandmothers who have seen
enough war to know what it means
to lose. They are daughters living
in a world teetering on the edge of time.

Duane Poncy, 54
Portland

the white path is the peace path, she said

take the white path
my grandmother said.
so I threw my old suitcase
into a Plymouth Valiant
moved to California
lost my okie drawl
lost my red skin
and married a white waitress.

take the white path, son
I repeated to my boy
as he tossed his sports bag
into his Jeep Cherokee
and went off like a brave
to join the army
to fight for black gold
and kill brown-skinned babies.

in a black body bag
I brought my little boy
back to Indian Country.
Grandmother, I said
the white path, it ain't
all it's cracked up to be.
well, you weren't listening, son
my old grandmother said.

now, ain't that how it goes.

Stephen Trent Potter, 43
Portland

Ordinary

They say I can't make a difference.
Being ordinary.
My common genes
Have walked a common path.
My plain face echoes plainly,
Those come before.
My heart beats the steady rhythm,
Of a steadfast way.
But what is it that stirs me now
Pulling to an uncommon depth?
What voice calls me now?
As I stand here now,
My heart beating in my throat
I sense
It is the ordinary me
That must make all the difference.

Back to the Cradle

This weekend, our tanks rolled into Baghdad.
Just south lies ancient Babylon
Called by some the "cradle of our civilization".
Thousands of years later
The 'most civil of us all'
Comes back 'home'.
What have we learned
Since our birth?
Now we try to reach God
With a pile of bombs
Instead of a pile of rocks

Amanda Powell and students
Eugene

"Tristes guerras" Miguel Hernández (Spain), 1910–1942

"Tristes guerras" is #57 of *Cancionero y romancero de ausencias*
(Songs and Ballads of Absence), 1938–1941, completed in prison
following the Spanish Civil War (1936–39). The translations are by
students of Spanish at the University of Oregon, in Amanda Powell's
workshop on Literary Translation.

TRISTES GUERRAS

Tristes guerras
si no es amor la empresa.
Tristes, tristes.

Tristes armas
si no son las palabras.
Tristes, tristes.

Tristes hombres
si no mueren de amores.
Tristes, tristes.

Miguel Hernández

Sad Wars

Wretched wars
if life is not love.
Sad, sad.

Treacherous weapons
if they are not the word.
Sad, sad.

Sad men
if they don't die of love.
Sad, sad.

translated by Olivier Clarinval

Unfortunate Wars

Unfortunate wars
if love is not the undertaking.
Unfortunate, unfortunate.

Unfortunate arms
if they are used instead of words.
Unfortunate, unfortunate.

Unfortunate humanity
if they do not die of love.
Unfortunate, unfortunate.

translated by Mary Larson

Sad Wars

Sad wars,
if love be not the company.
Sad, sad.

Sad arms,
if words be not the device.
Sad, sad.

Sad men,
if death be not of love.
Sad, sad.

translated by Sheerin Shahinpoor

Unfortunate Wars

Unfortunate wars
if love is not the enterprise.
What a shame.

Unfortunate weapons
if they are not words.
What a shame.

Unfortunate soldiers
if they do not die of love.
What a shame.

translated by Heather Valle-Torres

Sad Wars

Sad wars
when we are not striving for love.
Sad. Very sad.

Sad weapons
when we don't take aim with words.
Sad. Very sad.

Sad indeed
when it isn't love we die for.
Sad. Very sad.

translated by Amanda Powell

Frances Reed, 85
Portland

The Training

My son went off to war today!
He left when I was standing there;
I went inside, I thought to pray—
But couldn't find the words to say.

My gentle, sympathetic son
Who tends a wounded bird with care;
Who turns a plant to face the sun,
Is now prepared to shoot a gun.

He'll load his gun and shoot a man,
He'll fight for "Freedom Everywhere!"
He's trained to kill (and kill he can).
He's trained to hate—himself?

Susan Reese, 51
Portland

A Terrible Winter

Clutched lovingly in my hands,
a book, one of those hard to put down;
I will be bereft without its pages.
The end nears,
so I welcome a sound outside my window,
the report and rasp of a shovel being thrust
into dormant ground, my husband, digging.

Yesterday I, too, made my way into the soil,
digging six to eight inches,
planting bulbs, irises for spring,
finding sprouts already waiting

beneath a thin veneer of winter
like players ready to take the stage.

Meanwhile, UN inspectors search Iraq,
poking beneath another kind of surface,
digging for evidence of non-compliant
signs that evil or war lie in wait,
industrial strength buds impregnable
to the human cry for peace.

Boys and girls wait on ships,
on land, in the air,
brave faces and bold actions
over eggshell hearts and porcelain bodies,
naiveté to be sacrificed
like early buds to frost.

And in Oregon,
hopefully only sprouts
wait to burst through winter into spring,
and the only weapons are shovels
in loving hands,
because if the end nears I will be bereft,
each life a story I hope never ends,
each poised and ready to take the stage,
with so much to lose
just beneath the surface.

Vicki Reitenauer
Portland

Disturbances

        in the field known as March, moving
south to north: over the cause-
way, white flock falls
like dandruff onto the wrinkling
skin of lake. In Philadelphia, all of South

Street's shops have thrown
open their doors to the sacramental
breeze. Buzz of a tattoo
pen sweetens our common air. A child left
alone and locked
in a car hasn't stopped
finding the horn.

after Lynne Sharon Schwartz

Carlos Reyes
Portland

We Are Waiting for Peace to Break Out

—for Marvin Simmons

We are waiting for peace to break out
We are waiting for flowers to bloom
We are waiting for the moon to come
from behind the black clouds of war
We are waiting for the light
We are waiting
and as we wait we sings song of celebration
We are waiting
and as we wait we hold out our hands in love and friendship:
white hands extended in friendship to black hands
and brown and green hands of the earth
We are waiting
and while we wait we applaud those who have gone before us
preaching peace: all the Martin Luther Kings, all the Gandhis…
We are waiting for peace to break out
and as we wait we dance: we dance with the cold east wind
with the creaking singing branches of giant firs
we dance with the devils
of dust and the angels of clouds
We are waiting
and as we wait we are learning the language

of burning roses and the sunflowers slowly turning toward the sun
We are waiting for peace to break out
and while we wait we are learning to listen
to cries for mercy and cries for help
though we may not know the language
We are learning to listen for the arrival of doves
We are waiting for peace to break out
and while we wait we are smiling at you
at all of you—at the you and the me in the mirror...
We are waiting for peace to break out
We are waiting for buds to pop though it is deep winter
We wait for peace as patiently as the drop of water
on the lips at the mouth of the fountain
We wait knowing the water of peace is cool and sweet
sure that the crystal drop will fall on the earth
in spite of any of man's evil actions—

Kirsten Rian, 35
Portland

Interpretation

It's falling red today, at 2 am on
the west coast, which is 2:30 pm on the
Kyber Pass where, at any given moment,
the same stars could revolt against the sky
and shoot across my black, so thick
I'm tempted to reach out my hand as
I stand on my porch, just to see, just
to test the limits of interpreting a
moment like this. Across the world
you're counting red stones in a line,
spraying stones white for luck, and
side by side delineating fate. And it
can't be easy, choosing these stones.
And I don't know how you do it. And
I finally feel cold enough to go back inside,

my day has crossed yours, and midnight
lingered long past; but before I do,
I throw one last question into the sky:
if you tossed one of those red stones across
the top of one of those still lakes you
told me about, deep in the meadows inside
the Hindu Kush where light sticks
to the surrounding hills, would it skip?

Tom Riker, 66
Oregon Coast

Two Way Streets

The coming of the tanks
Smelling of oil and rust
Soon to smell of blood…
Then
The bombed out, lost refugees
Carrying their children
Burying their dead by the roadside
Without flowers or good-byes.

Comes the soldiers and guns
New, young faces eager for glory
& colored ribbons that decorate
Their chests.
Leaving behind empty towns & old people
Sitting in broken chairs
Watching tanks and smoke.

Count the tears and screams
Pile up the dead and broken dreams.

Emily Dawn Riley, 23
Portland

It's Timing, Mister

we live in a time
where the threat of a nuclear attack seems imminent at times
and I fear genocide more
than naturally occurring diseases or drunk driving.
this war is not stopping,
this Star Wars sequel,
"America Strikes Back,"
good ole America,
with its Bible belt and big pot belly.

we live in a time
where I can't distinguish anymore just who the hell is the terrorist
and who the hell isn't.
what do you care?
somebody's bombing somebody out there beyond the ocean,
on the distant burning horizon,
and people run for cover from the falling sky
and whir of the war planes close overhead.

we live in a time
where everyone at anytime could be caught in the crosshairs
and everyone at anytime is ready to fire.
who are you aiming your psychic missiles at, mister?
mister America,
who are you anyways?
and who's going to tell you when it's the Right time to end this
    mess?
I want to know what will be LEFT when the RIGHT time happens.
mister cocaine college boy
mister daddy's boy presidente
mister anthrax incorporated.
mister America,
what's that white powder doing all over your nose and in our
    mailboxes?

we live in a time
where the presidency is a crock of shit
and the vice Cheney is living in hiding,
and nobody knows whether or not it's a great time
to just take a sick day from work for life.

we live in a time
when patriotism is just a marketing strategy
for Chevy trucks and newsmen.
all the real Patriots died long ago
with the red white and blue bleeding like an old tattoo from
    their tattered hearts.
now patriotism and pride only breed contempt for those
    exempt
from our special little deal with America.
so what's on your patriotic bonus check, mister?
when are you going to tell me about your next dirty deal?

we live in a time
running in rewind,
pulling us like a record needle across the worn out patterned
    grooves
of clever politics
and camera happy presidents.

mister America
mister America,
Hey! I love you
like I don't love any other mister.

mister America,
we live in a time that is not ours.
mister America,
this is timed living,
ticking down the last seconds until destruction.
we are living on your time,
mister America,
wishing for better but placing our bets on the worst,

we are yours,
and not our own.

Julie Rogers, 45
Ashland

Dreaming of Peace

Comparing my life to those in Iraq
I find nothing to complain about
yet, no bombs have dropped
on our turf, rumor of war
like a blimp above the city,
a neon message blinking in fog
above a skyline richly lit
and a freeway full of traffic.

That sound I have never heard,
ground blasting open,
a playground, an office building.
Is it hard to imagine
the impact, this house knocked off
its foundation, these walls stripped away,
perhaps our bodies
found later in the rubble?

This street like any other,
these neighbors.
We eat and nod off to the news.
Tonight I will stay up late,
say my prayers
and go to sleep
thinking we are safe.
I will dream.

Picture This
for Ani Baba

The picture of peace
is drawn with a finger
of bone, pointing
away from this body.
We will leave it behind.

First the beauty droops, muscle slack
as cut rope, the slide of skin,
wilting sex, then the mind
closes down.

In the face of death we fear
to be alone, unlike the way
we try to abandon pain
believing it is someone
to be rid of: wife/husband
daughter/son, enemy/friend,
calling it by name, wanting
to believe that if it is yours
it is not mine.

We hold our bodies
like shadows, as briefly
as the slap of a hand or a fist
unfolding. Yet how we squirm
when feeling, nervous
with compassion, so much
stranger than desire, so unfamiliar
to want for others,
to live for them.

Camille Roman
Portland

sky in war

the sun and moon
          hang,
                    mouths
                         screaming
     in the war-streaked
     sky today

Jerry Rooney, 67
<u>Corvallis</u>

Acts of Faith

It's an act of Faith
To wake up in the morning and expect to find Someone next
    to you.

To turn on a water faucet.
To drop a letter in the mailbox.
These too are Acts of faith.

To write on your calendar.
Dial the phone.
Plant a garden.

Acts of faith.

To check your calendar.
Floss your teeth.

Acts of faith.

To have a child.
Write a word.

Acts of faith.

To believe in a god.
In heaven.
In Love.
Life.

Or
Yes,
In
Peace...

Ann Ross, 41
Portland

Shame

An arrogant stride
The doctrine of pre-emption
Old Liberty weeps

Harley Sachs, 72
Portland

Bayonet Practice

Bayonet practice in the dusty chapel yard—
The Sergeant with his circle of nameless recruits
Drills
In the chapel, the organist
Practicing hymns for Sunday
Trills
Today is not Sunday

By the numbers, the armed circle advances
"Parry— thrust— Smash!"
In thirsty dust we drill
To the organ's funeral march,
Kill! Kill!

— *Recollections of Camp Breckinridge, 1953*

Ralph Salisbury, 77
Eugene

Green Smoke

"Helicopters?" he asks, long distance. But
I'm Heavy Bombers, It's six in the morning, not nine.
I am Pacific, and he's Atlantic. It's World
War Two again, my sleep destroyed

By rescuers, seeking to rescue one of their own—
A crew-mate with my same name—from oblivion,

And, yes, eighteen, I saved eight men,
Nine if I count myself,
Corralling a bomb banging wild like a colt
Against our own bomb-bay, and now I'm a poet
And try to save everything
I love. But, no;
Grass bursts like green smoke up
From graves of some friends,
And only my best wishes go
To The Rescue Squadron Reunion.

We Are Asked to Understand,

the barman, who's heard it before, and me,
a stranger, ex-soldier, my worst not so bad as this
pilot's, his rocket the same,
to men in a tank, as my friends' bombing plane,
what turned them into meat and cooked it, but
my memory is smoke, vanishing in wind.

Two ears hear,
and two once more,

that a mouth, which had said
what all men say
to sweethearts and wives, spurted blood as hot
as come into crotch,

that, his friend's severed head
between drenched thighs,
our brother has got to keep on flying and shooting
and living the horror, the guilt, the grief
all of us live—or should—
our dead born and born again and again in our brains.

Francesca Sanders, 50
Portland

Vagrant

I saw the woman. Clearly.

"She had no home" you would say. You would say she was a
beggar. You would curl up your fleshy hands in your pockets
and walk by.

"She is a homeless person, a vagrant" you would say.

And then you would walk into a restaurant and eat platters of
spaghetti. "What fine wine," you would say.

I saw a different person seated calmly on the street. The
woman I saw most certainly had a home. Yes, it was miles away
but I could see it clearly.

It was in Baghdad. A beautiful home, dirt floor swept clean
every day. Little ones were playing in their shirts, which had
been beaten with a switch and then washed in the cool stream.

It was a beautiful home before the Texan walked in and tore it
down. Spurs on his heels, he smashed everything of beauty and
sent her on your way.

Her children were lost. "What for?" she wondered? "It's not
for you to say," she tells herself.

I see this woman not homeless, but instead carrying her home on her back. Finally making her way through the streets of America for where else can she go?

Yes, she still cowers at the sound of cowboy boots scraping the sidewalk. She winces at the people making their way in to eat their pasta.

But inside, her head is held high for in her mind's eye, she is sweeping a spotless hut. Her soul is clean and so she still knows how to smile.

Maxine Scates

Vanishing

New leaves droop in the field,
domain of one old oak drenched
by a passing shower—wasps waken
deep in the undercurrent of woodpiles,
men and women bend in their yards
                as they did another spring.

Till and stake, twilight hazy, singular
with expectation of the coming summer
when driving through last light
down this loved road, news broke
through the collage of feature stories
I wasn't listening to—somewhere
we were bombing, casual, retailiatory,
what we'd grown used to as our right.

It was May because irises bloomed,
shimmered, iridescent,
and then the echo behind each thing
I'd sometimes heard
was no longer background but foreground
something always known, the way

one of those women bent in her yard
might straighten because she feels a numbing
in her arm as the sledge hammer of pain speeds
toward her heart, a shattering
        as dusk disintegrated,
drift and swirl,
rejoining in a larger shape
so big we had not seen it: the devil
in a medieval fresco
inhaling beauty, exhaling
tiny human bodies tumbling, slack—
and we were both the demon and the fallen,
what we could only see elsewhere
there with us, organic,
as the rising smell of mint
from the fields on this road
on a hot August day. Our road,
the road we built, our careless road.

Judith Sawyer, 59
Eugene

Endgame

Pundits and politicians assail the air
with scare talk, loosing the dogs of war...
As though we needed to shed more blood
to honor our wounds—then dub our killing "collateral damage,"
to barter free speech, basic rights, due process,
pandering to the latest "patriot" game.

Small men puffed with power were weaned on that game,
laughing as they waved toy guns in the air,
"Cowboys and Indians" part of the killing process,
their rite of passage, until they saw everything in terms of war,
be it football, sex, or drugs, not reckoning the damage,
the demand to shed more blood.

Who would have thought that others had so much blood
in them? But what do we care when it's only a video game
in another country, where we can't see the damage
to luckless children, men, and women breathing air
tainted with the stink and squalor of war,
where there's no such thing as due process?

What of our own complicity in a political process
that calls us to sanction spilling blood
of people whom we know not, in a war
that spans a world of our own making, with no endgame
in sight; that till it recoils on us, will still wear an air
of unreality? When will we begin to face the damage?

When will those on whom we've rained death turn that damage
back on us tenfold, in the age-old process
of revenge and retribution, until the very air
cries out in agony: No more blood!
Pundits and politicians, it's time to call the game
and nevermore prate "glory," "honor," "justice" in the name of war.

To call for hope, that we may mute the cry for war,
knowing no one ever died for glory, only damage.
To bury our need to play the murderous game.
To nurture wisdom instead of warriors, and the harder process
of growing up. To finally understand: all people share one blood
and yearn to breathe the same untainted air.

So let us put an end to war, begin the healing process,
Do no more damage that must be paid in blood
Banish the vicious game that we may freely breathe the life-
      sustaining air.

Charles Seluzicki
Portland

For the Iraqi Dead

Wind need not know
Its way,
Nor the sand that gathers into dunes

Dew, like sand, flies up
In mist,
Gathers in a well at midnight

Two days now and a bucket
Lies empty by the well,
Wind fills it with sounds of mourning

Alice Shapiro, 56
Florence

A Quartet of Limericks for Laura

1.
I know that you respect your spouse
And you want some peace in the Whitehouse
But if free speech you will save
Then please do be brave
And speak like a lion, not a mouse.

2.
It's about freedom of speech
Our Bill of Rights grants that to each
We won't be quiet
Expect us to riot
Until the world truly does
Live in peace.

3.
I feel that it is sacred duty
To always promote peace and beauty

Poetry symposium or no
The movement will go
'til your spouse does stop acting so snooty.

4.
Oh there is a first lady named Laura
Who did something that I abhor-a
She cancelled the poets
It seems she don't know it
But the pen is mightier than the sword-a

Myrna Shepper, 65
Corvallis

Grieving

I see the flag at half mast
my eyes fill with tears
catching me with surprise
realising my liquid eyes
are for all we've lost
not just a space shuttle.
I weep for my country
about those who wish to harm us
also for those we wish to harm.
What has happened to my America?
from the liberators of the death camps
to the bully of the world
I weep
for the people on the streets
Who we cannot house
for the hungry
Who we cannot feed
for the sick
We cannot heal
While we spend money for war
I weep for my country
for the vision that seems lost
Oh America the beautiful
Who shed it's light on thee.

Steven Shinn, 50
<u>Eugene</u>

Heron's Lament

Ever seen the
    Great Blue Heron
              take flight
    from the reeds
    along the river,
Fly almost   out   of   sight
    then bank left
    and return
    gliding,
        skimming,
    just above the rippling rapids,
    drop its spindle legs,
    fold its umbrella wings and
Stop   without hesitation?

Pure
    eloquent
        grace.

Life could be
    could have been
Marvelous
    like that
    in so many ways.

Magnificent
    like sunrise
    over frosted tree tops,
Or sunset
    over vast ocean waves.

Glorious
    like the birth
    of a wanted child,
    and the smile
    on that child's face.

But the Heron's been watching me
    and sadly cries
For the young child
    in my mind is part of an old story
    known by all wise creatures.

The folly
    of the human experiment.

Beings granted
    the capacity for
    creativity
    compassion
    and love,
But not willing
    to control
    their power.

Short sighted
    self-serving
    greedy bastards
Incapable of recognizing
    the simple truth
That we are all
    connected.

There are no separate
    races
    creeds
    nationalities
No separate sexes
    genders
    sexualities.

Indeed,
    no separate species
Just *beings*
    belonging to each other
    and to the planet
    which gave them birth.

It's going to get worse
        before it gets better
                        if it gets better.

The tyrants
        have squared off again.
Each one
        wants it all
        for himself.

So we will fight again
        kill again,
        be maimed
        and die again
For them.

Maybe what we should be
        thinking about
Is the post Apocalypse
Assuming, of course,
                there is one.

Maybe then
        we'll be ready
        to work together
        live together
Provide for the
        common good
Provide so that
        every
                living
                        thing
        can find
        and reach
        its potential.

The Heron blinks at me.
We both know
        we're only dreaming
About how glorious life
        could have been.

Bill Shively, 50
<u>Newberg</u>

The Explosives Are for the Stumps

The explosives are for the stumps

We have been on the barricades before
We have torn down
We have blown up
We have had revolutions and joined civil war
Family fights
Some of us have struck our fathers
Some of us have left our mother
We have been on the barricades before

She hands me a brick
I feel the heft and edge
The potential is huge and the rage
Is rooted and thick

What has happened has happened
To us: we have survived to this end

With the brick I want to build
A foundation waist deep in the mud
With battens holding back the earth and
Jacks holding up the shed
With Eliades Ochoa singing along

He hands me a club
It's crooked shaft and gnarled head
Light in flight
Yet stout enough to fend off blows
And I want to build
A fire to warm the neighbors that gather
In the wane to share stories about
Their families and lies about their
Histories with these
Cuvees of earth from Doug's winery

The explosives are for the stumps
The underground press is all poetry and fiction
We have tried changing it
From the inside
And we have tried quitting

We have been on the barricades before
We have torn down
We have blown up
We have had revolutions and joined civil war
Family fights
Some of us have struck our fathers
Some of us have left our mother

And most of us you can count on
If it comes down to that
Again.

We have been on the barricades before.

01-01-01

Jim Shugrue, 54
Portland

On A Photograph of a Severed Hand

What is the sound of one hand
lying in the middle of a road
waving goodbye to its lost body?

How has it come this far from a hand
to mouth existence? How did it earn
its crust of callus? Is this

the right hand or the left? I cannot
tell. This is a photograph of a hand;
they could print it either way.

I've never seen a hand, alone,
open and empty in the middle
of a road, and pray to the god

they tell me has us all
in his good hands never to see one.
I know what history is. Our hand-

me-down bodies are mostly water,
and we spend them in tears and sweat.
Here is my hand. Take it,

and give me yours, while we
are still attached.

Terry Simons
Portland

i met a woman yesterday

who informed
me "there will
always be war"

who informed me
"they are all
bad people"

who grew angry
at my protestations
and walked away

who did not want
to hear me or see me
or make love

who made me see
we are chained to
this brutal thing

Bill Siverly, 59
Portland

The Prince of Darkness

Smug in his steely seersucker suit,
Black eyes flashing supreme conviction,
The well-fed gourmand tears himself away from table,
Long enough to hector the dupes of détente
Who dream of Soviet threat will one day disappear.

Stuffed with facts and stats and bravado,
He argues nonchalantly that SALT II has failed:
Both sides continue building nukes and counter-nukes,
So "arms control" proves no control at all,
And the U.S. might as well break out before the Russians do.

He fails to mention that he himself
As aide to Senator Boeing in seventy-nine
Planned the Senate defeat of the very agreement
He now claims has failed. Meanwhile
Both sides have observed core terms of SALT II.

Indeed, both sides continue building
Arsenals of doom, like SS-25, MX and cruise,
But now they are reaching the limits of equity,
The day the race should end,
Exactly foreseen by those who designed the treaty.

Reagan and his men talk arms control,
But they don't want to end the race:
They have money to make and power to take
By means of large corporations committed
To the next generation of weapons only.

So Reagan and his men send Richard Perle,
Assistant Minister of Fear and hatchet man,
Intellectual servant of hate and aggression,
To bully the Senate committees into submission:
To disagree with him renders comfort to the Russians.

The view from his Washington office window
Seems less real to Perle than the numbers in his brain;
He never sees the world out here,
The Phoenix Fire of sunrise, birdsong, and pokeweed,
Where humans can be generous, charming, and kind.

Worse for us than the epidemic of AIDS,
Worse than the African famine, than deforestation,
Worse than ozone depletion or any pollution,
Worse than a hundred death squads of oppression,
Richard Perle would risk our total annihilation.

Mandelstam said the people remember their enemy:
May Richard Perle go down among those who go hungry
So leaders can buy the weapons they want to deploy.
May Richard Perle go down to warmonger hell:
Nothing to eat but peace and good will.

Bryan Smith, 27
Portland

all this madness, it's

when all the leaders have gone mad
and then been re-elected
when it's the biologists that are endangered
and the auditors are paper millionaires

what is there left to do?
where is there left to move?
who will you blame?
who can you possibly shame?

it's all clogging the freeways
it's all stuck in the drain
it's the fine print in your insurance
saying good samaritans stay away

where are my brothers and sisters?
    are they inside those tinted SUV's?
are they behind those gated trophy homes?
with pills to keep the conscience at bay?

what the people want is an answer
and what they get is the score
they say they want spirituality
then they search at the store

they want to repent
by the light of the moon
they want forgiveness
from every grassy knoll

but this feeling comes
and then it goes
faster than a church bell's toll

Deb Smith, 44

In Memory of Robert McAfee Brown

Crisis-bred craving,
our arms ache for loved ones--
tight comfort of embrace
as the water batters or the
lava flows.
But Hiroshima turns me
and my hand meets empty air.

Neither Truth nor Consequences

War should not be
a sleight-of-hand.
Afghanistan—
now you see it,
now you don't.
Didn't find Osama,
but have we got a show for you!

War should not be
a sound-bite.
"We have freed them!"
as the camera steadily pans away,
indifferent to the fact that
Power abhors a vacuum.
Looking fixedly away,
no care for who or what rushes
"freely" in.

War should not be
a re-election strategy.
Does ANYONE really believe
Saddam more evil now
than when we sold him arms?

There may indeed be a time for war,
but last and sorrowful—
all just solutions tried and
crumbled to dust,
back pushed to the bloody wall of
life and death.

No one should die as
fodder
for numbers in a poll.

Walter Smith, 56
Joseph

The State of the Union

Heav'n has no rage, like love to hatred turn'd,
Nor Hell a fury, like a woman scorned.
        (William Congreve, 1697)

John Milton, the blind guide, said with glee:
"And in thy right hand lead with thee
The mountain nymph, sweet Liberty."

Our fathers she seduced and bore
This nation on a distant lore.

Two centuries of mirth she birthed,
And continents of confidence.

While new embraces took our breath
Retreating phantoms coiled fine lace
Upon imagination's race
To retrofit the ship of state—
For transporting 'the better sort'
To bliss the Lady'd never sport—
And sail'd it toward the lemming curse
Collapsing cultures drive to verse.

And now she slips our flaccid grasp
And tempts our whole United States
To love those antiquated fates
Imposed upon the nation late
Deserting self-destructive tastes.

Invisible Hands

Citizens brown, alien, black,
Red, grey and yellow, well and ill:

Remember white girls and white boys
Believed the red hot rhetoric—
An empire of equality!

And they believed blue promises
All corporations freely use
To plumb the depths of servile souls
Who claim to lift all sinking boats by
Deploying trickle down ideas.

Such promises, ideas and rhetoric
Are pretty tools from an old kit
Ventriloquists use to affect,
To cloud the mind and steal the wit,
With antique priestly etiquette.

James Snowden, 37
Portland

Real Deal

This is not a war we fight
The enemy is ourselves
We fight for healthy behavior
Not for more blood

We need a new framework
Where we are still free
To be weird and wonderful
To create and express

Where people who are unhealthy
Are treated, monitored and healed
Not jailed or bombed

Even when it may take many lifetimes

Why can we be jailed for a joint
When someone is commended for killing
Or rapes the environment
It doesn't make sense

Big brother might want to watch
The details with a closer eye
His views need to become healthy
For this country to grow

Be soft on the outside
And strong on the inside
Adaptation, flexibility and love
Are the real deal

Lisa Steinman, 53
Portland

The Old Woman's Poem

All summer the crows yelled at me from trees
in praise of the immaterial. Surly
I was by fall. The laundramat sign read:

"Re-grand opening." And the world did open,
garden notebooks filling with weeds—
meadow rue, lady's mantle, the first page

left blank for Elijah. Just in case. Though
the papers lamented the weapons of mass
destruction, as if destruction did not

occur to us one by one. Now passing
cars sing in warm rain, but not well, what with
their tin ears, petulant and off-kilter.

I wake up with a furrowed heart. I am
as cultivated as the delicate
smell of carrots thinned early. I can taste

my childhood. Look: a small figure dances
in the yard. No, look: it's me. No, I'm here
rehearsing the dance in memory, trying

to imagine an older woman's life.
Somehow I've come to feel such an untoward
affection for my younger self, I could

just cry. Instead, I thin carrots, hearing
crows, living carefully ... as if I might
otherwise forget to wake, eat, breathe.

Leah Stenson, 54
Portland

My Father

In a childhood photograph my father appears as a skinny boy
with sunken eyes holding a cut out of a paper moon. A Gentile
in a neighborhood of Jews, he would light the stoves of the
faithful on Sabbath eves. During the war, the Nazis shot his
plane down. He bailed out and his parachute became entangled
in a tree, his feet barely touching the ground. The Nazis cut him
loose and put him in a POW camp where he decoded messages
and plotted the escape of comrades. As an intelligence officer,
he was bound by duty to remain behind. In the camp, they
usually ate cereal with worms, but one day some prisoners
bribed the Nazis for a chicken. He refused to eat it. He refused
to eat chicken for the rest of his life.

Sharon Streeter, 59
Portland

Dear George W.

Please tell us when you're
going to drop the big one. I'll be tuned
to CNN or MSNBC. I could even buy a second set
so I won't miss a thing. It will be more grand than towers tumbling
to the ground. No people falling, though. Instead, they'll maybe bounce into
the air? or just be running fast, their hair on fire? Will we see them screaming?
See their body parts? What will we see, George? Will we hear their wails?
What will we hear, George? Will we feel?
I don't know, George, this will be
a television
first.
I wouldn't
miss it
for the world,
unless,
of course,
it's not
prime time,
or it
should
drop
on me
and
my
TV.

Sharon E.
Streeter,
citizen in despair

D. L. Sutton, 53
Portland

War

Such a small word, yet powerful and fierce,
With results that reflect on each side.
We can't help but ask, is there any other way,
Is there anything that we haven't tried?

Can we settle the conflicts without shedding blood?
Without tearing our Country apart?
Is it possible to win without firing a shot?
Can we end it before it does start?

Could there be a solution, somewhere out there,
That could Unite us all as to one?
We search for answers and it's there in the Word,
There is a way it can be done!

We must be ready to fall on our knees,
And, on our face we must March to the Throne,
Forgiveness is still a part of our Life,
Lets Pray before the first stone.

Prayer is the Answer we're searching for now,
So let's Pray for the World and its scars.
War only leads to sorrow and hurt,
Without Sin, the Victory is ours!

AMERICA BLESS GOD!

03-03-03

Lisa Taylor, 25
Corvallis

Thoughts on Pictures

In the news paper there is a picture.
There will come many more in the days that follow,
Each bringing a story
Or
Do you see an enemy?

The lady walking through the market,
baby in her arms,
Small child clinging to her skirt,
she looks sad-worried.
She searches for food to feed her family;
perhaps some veggies to put into a stew for dinner tonight.

We will bomb her too?
She minds her business and goes about her daily life.
We would kill her?
She struggles to live peacefully under Saddam's rule;
beneath a political leader we call a tyrant?

The eyes of this woman, so anxious
Wondering what will become of her children
They stay in my mind.

It is a true conviction.
I cannot stand by and silently watch as those around me
prepare for war
They do as they are told-like dogs.
With out questioning who this war will benefit.
It is not for me, not in my name.

Maria, the daughter of migrant farm workers
who worked their fingers to the bone to make ends meet
My cousin, who thought the reserves would be a great way for
her to get a

college education,
a chance at the American dream.

She was forced to drop out of the University last week
They shipped her off to D.C.
From there she does not know if she will go to North Korea
or Iraq
She only knows that she will not return intact.
Whether that means

Dismemberment
Or
Apart from her consciousness
I only know she will not return as I knew her.

They send the poor to kill the poor
In the name of power, money and greed:
Words of which the poor have never known the full meaning.

Karin Temple, 61
Astoria

Tillamook Air Museum

The behemoth beckoned
for eons
dwarfing cows
in pacific pastures
until I came
to pay for a neck-craning
view of the vault.
Zeppelins extinct,
the hangar is home now
to scores of
war birds
gayly arrayed

in rows with legends.
Winter chill invades
when I encounter
a companion of old,
Angst
of enemy air raids.

First words
of the child of war:
Mutti, Tata, Bombalarm.
No sleep is safe
from the wailing
of sirens,
struggles with buttons
and shoelaces,
staccato
of running feet.
From my blanket cocoon
I mark the migration
by tunnel lights
overhead.
Heavy tread
wears down the stone steps
to the Bunker where
my mother pitches her songs
against the rumble and roar
of planes
waxing and waning
in black-out skies.
I learn my lullabies
to rocking walls
and a basso continuo
of fear.

There is no nostalgia
in war
if you have ever
been bombed.

Andrew Tully, 35
Portland

War Bonnet Sonnet

War makes nothing happen.
It's good-God for no dog;
cats hate it more than me.
Violence suggests the end
of existence. Animals treat
each other better than us.
Guns and drums take up space
where books could be read,
upside down and to each other.
Forget flags and ships,
kiss me on the lips instead.
It beats hell out of shooting
bottles and caps until we're dead.
Politicos make me think red

David Vest

Heavy Weather Rolling In

Thunder rolling from the east, dark clouds across the west
Whatever cards you're holding, fold 'em to your chest
There's a siren and a searchlight gnawing at the sky
In the middle of the city, heard a mountain lion cry
And I can feel it in the wind, heavy weather rolling in

Baby's on the highway, can't call her on the phone
Whatever's coming her way, she'll have to handle it alone
It's gonna be a bad one, knocked all the power out
It's the kind of storm the Bible and the gypsies talk about
Watch out my friend, heavy weather rolling in

Try to fly below the radar, cross your name off every list
The guardians will tell you that it's useless to resist
Every time you watch a movie, every time you make a call
Every time you write a letter, they wanna know about it all
Here it comes again, heavy weather rolling in

Better not drive the main roads, hole up in your room
Welcome to the city of the howling doomed
It's all for your own safety, it's all for your own good
Nobody would ever hurt you here, not unless they could
That's right my friend, some heavy weather rolling in

God made it rain one time for 40 days and 40 nights
This time they gonna let it rain until they get it right
No use calling your mama, she's low down and dejected
Can't call the president, he's already disconnected
Feels like the time of the end, heavy weather rolling in

Morris Walker
Corvallis

How Do I Pray for Peace

How do I pray for Peace, oh Lord
In a world that's gone insane?
When all else fails in rhyme and reason
and we ask for Peace in your name?

Do I just say, Lord please give us Peace?
Do I promise my love and that's it?
Does it come with a joyous flood cross the land,
and we wait and we pray and we sit?

What do you need from the cowering masses
to let you know we want Peace?
How do I pray for Peace dear Lord,
for I know that it's yours to give?

But I see the unthinkable happening now,
and we pray because that's what we're taught.
But how do I know that Peace will come at all,
If prayer is all that we've got?

Do I go deep within, to that silent place
where you seem to be everywhere?
Do I settle my worried mind down
and find that elusive Peace there?

Are you giving me answers to the questions I ask?
Is it here that it all begins, where consciousness stops
and solitude reigns and the battles turn to soft gentle winds.
Where there is no fight except to be quiet
and by not fighting yourself you are calm?

Is this how I pray for Peace my God?
Because if it is, then I have just one prayer,
that I feel the billions of Peace seeking souls,
in harmony, join me there.

Frank Walkingfeather

on preparing for war

the world
torn and mutilated

the broken bird song
            (no i am not a target
but
bit by bit i am destroyed)

Margareta Waterman
Winston

poetry and the american voice

insult: warlords condescend to speak of poetry
lend us your magic, o poets, to serve our propaganda

every day, in the paper
in any town in this country

every day, in the paper
degradation of language so horrific

no word can mean anything
because public words

are so far
from ever meaning what they say

we all know these lies are lies
we read this newspeak, find the hidden facts

we all know that this government wasn't honestly elected
that it has no respect for us, no interest

in the public interest

that greed beyond sanity is its only value
we all know what the papers don't dare print

but don't expect poets
whose life is language and the clean use of words

to contribute to the hypocrisy

Lisa Wells, 20
<u>Portland</u>

the inevitable

we watched as the starry eyed monster stirred
quiet from the crook of his arm
low lying, soft kneed

held breaths tight
wrapped in memory of that same damn seed
not just by history books
or projected loss graphs,
not by 1960s time magazines.
but by a deeper memory

we are still holding

[a memory from the gut
an ancestral whisper]

we remember the day when counting coup fell by the way of a
new sort of war.

extermination.

his stirring gives to waking.
senses gathering.
we know he will wake.
we know what's coming.
we know it doesn't matter much to breath
and so step out
grieving eloquence for the earth beneath him.

Ingrid Wendt, 58
Eugene

Words of Our Time

And have our tongues always not known what they speak?
Good students, smart as whips, always
hitting the books before killing the lights

Armed with knowledge, and struck by new ideas, who wasn't
proud to take stabs at it,
    firing off questions like shots in the dark.

Dead right, dead wrong,
there was always a time we could talk without thinking of
    dressing to kill. Drowning our sorrows.

Parties were blasts, or they bombed.
No joke was ever caught dead without
its punch line.

And here is a time when a president says
    we still have a shot at peace
        and the surest way to peace is through war

When the media says
    fire that kills you is friendly
    when it's from your own side

When those who say
    they want the troops to stay alive
    are told they don't support them

In this time when words
can make any war just
        and peace, a smashing success

In this time, words
like feathers
    knock some of us over

And some of us stand
    speechless.

January 1991

Freedom Williams, 26
<u>Portland</u>

World War 3

in an arid desert
thousands of realities away
encompassed by a people
with which we cannot relate
and ruled
by a lie so vast
that the end is merely speculation

and next door
a man we call president
volunteers our children for war
a war fought in the bowels
of a
gas tank
and justified by a modern-day
dictator
from behind the wheel of an suv

papa would be proud
as the doe-eyed masses
head out
oblivious to the truth
that hangs over them
amidst the black clouds
that hang loosely from a sky
just trying to survive

the fight

a country
sucked in
by the proverbial vacuum
of deceit
hanging their hopes on a cowboy
disguised as a leader
while the self-proclaimed patriots
reject
the former warriors
that line the streets
made ragged by the reality of yesterday's war
begging for compassion
or a coin
and haunted by their memories
of a time when
they could still feel the sidewalk
beneath their feet
a time when
their land loved them like brothers
a time when
the distorted faces of unknowing children
buried under the all-encompassing
horror of a napalm blanket
did not haunt them
in the throes of their midnight sleep

when will we learn
that hate
is counter-productive
and that raising the flag
of intimidation
only paves the road of demise
and when will we realize
the simplicity
and ease
of declaring war
from a bunker buried in a world
far below the rest of us

a man
disingenuous
unaffected

by lives
beyond the borders of his control
as though a zip code
identifies
who may live
and who may die
as though royalty
can ever sympathize
with poverty

i refuse to believe the answer lies
buried
in the sand of some foreign land
or in the metallic tip
of a warhead
as it races towards earth
headed for its final destination
the final solution
tearing through the living room
of a family
much like yours
just sitting down for dinner

the nameless
faceless
enemy
is a child
staring mournfully
at the pile of rocks
once a home
now a graveyard
for the only family he has ever known
a child
alone
a child we call
collateral damage

a battle fought
with an opponent
weaker than ourselves
by a government
reveling in its authority
its richness
its fortune

a battle fought against humanity
by a nation oblivious
to mortality

there will be no bloodshed
on my dime
there will be no blind allegiance this time
this battle may wage on
in spite of it all
but never by these hands
and
not
in
my
name

Hannah Wilson, 74
Eugene

State of the Union, 2003

A bag
a plastic bag
dun, crumpled
and curled,
turns out to be
a cat
dying,

abandoned or
dragged on its own
knowing
to lie down
in brush
by the running trail,

its Himalayan coat,
winter grass spun
into fluff.

Evelyn says,
I hope no one
mistakes me,
for a plastic bag.

Up ahead,
hollow drum
beats on the sawdust path,
a squad of boots,
camouflage and cadenced calls:

I'll tell you a ta - ale
I'll tell you a ta - ale
Of an airborne ra - n - ger
of an airborne ra - n- ger
Found himself in he - ll
found himself in he - ll.

David Wodtke, 42
Corvallis

Agreeable discord

Looking for how
the occasion of when
to seem is to know
this decision of whim

Now frank is abstruse
honesty lies
sharply obtuse
as compliance defies

secure is unsure
if meaning is mean

liberation war or
pure love unclean

health is disease
unity divisive
slavery release
ambivalence decisive

killing is kind
greed charity
sight is blind
common caring a rarity

leaders talk and say
nothing to listeners who don't
during darkness all day
of plentiful want.

The many are few
Who go when they come:
the false and the true.
Deaf dances with dumb.

Gaea Yudron, 61
<u>Ashland</u>

Making Peace

You don't have to be a poet to know
How many wars have been fought since your birth
Everywhere, from the unspoken
agonies of the family hearth
to bloody massacres in countries far away,
So many wars,
one cannot even be expected to list them all
or know how many have died.
And with each war, the wounded, the dead,
and those left to live on
In the ruins of whatever life once went on there,

holding in their heart the memory
of the particular beauties of the place,
which has been tortured
into unnatural way stations of the soul.

You don't have to be a poet to know
how many deaths you are complicit in
even when you never agreed
to any of those wars from the day of your birth.
Even if you grieve for nameless people
Roomfuls of them lying covered with dust in
some village in Africa, or out along
the roadside forgotten and ignored.

Some people will tell you, "Oh, that's
the human struggle,
that's the way life is,
there will always be war."
But do you buy it? Do you gradually
erode your spirit
into that political propaganda?

I do not want to use wars
as a marker of my lifespan,
even in the midst of this age,
known as the Kali Yuga.
It may be an age of Darkness,
but one is free to choose another way.
One does not have to be
a recognized holy person
to choose another way.
Any one of us can do it.

You don't have to be a magician to know
that the Presidency is no longer real.
Perhaps it never was.
At JFK's assassination,
you may have suspected that
some sleight of hand was at work.
Every 4 years I pray for a worthy candidate,

yet no one ever appears who is big enough
to do the job up right. Am I praying to conjure
a world that doesn't exist yet? You bet I am.

So a President who was never really elected,
who slipped through the gates using passwords,
kin, influence, completing an egregious victory,
why isn't a Greek drama written yet about it,
he, most likely insecure in his domain,
clamoured for war from the beginning.
It's the Taliban terrorists, it's Saddam Hussein,
The guy his father never finished off. It's oil.
It's a kind of impotence, a terrible impoverishment.
It's fear. The corruption of power.
You don't have to be
a great philosopher to know this.

The other day, a woman in
a Grandmother's Council told us
that she had a photo of George W. Bush on her altar.
Many people gasped in surprise. Why?
We all need praying over.
What will become of us if we
pray for the well-being
of our opponents,
if we gaze into their eyes
if we open ourselves
into a moment of peace and love.

Some people will tell you that
it's useless, impossible.
But are you going to buy that?
Some people will tell you that the only good
Indian is a dead Indian,
or Persian, or Jew, or Iraqi, or Moslem, or Bosnian, or Serb, or
    Croatian, or Huutu,
but are you going to believe that?

Index of Poets

About the Cover Art

Cover art is by Portland artist, writer and poet, Roberta Badger, who seeks to exemplify the interconnectedness of life and art.

Composition on War and Peace incorporates five acrylic paintings with the central theme of choices: peace and beauty represented by flowers, or war and violence represented by bombs and scenes of conflict and violation. The central image, "Peace 1945, the Promise," features the peace rose developed at the end of World War II as a living symbol for an end to all wars. It shows the promise of peace amidst contemporary and historical challenges to peace. Surrounding images are a four-part series entitled "Flowers and Bombs: Multicultural Tapestries". The flowers and floral designs are culturally relevant to each culture represented; the bombs and missiles are historically accurate portrayals of those used during the first Gulf War. From left top, going clockwise, "Oriental Cultures, New World Cultures, Indigenous Cultures, and Old World Cultures" portray four culturally distinct ways we understand and experience our world as we choose paths of war or peace, destruction or life, violence or beauty.

"Flowers and Bombs: Multicultural Tapestries" (acrylic on paper, 22 X 30" each, unframed) and "Peace 1945, the Promise" (acrylic on paper, 22 X 30" unframed) have had several Portland exhibitions.